How to Negotiate Like a Child

UNLEASH THE LITTLE MONSTER WITHIN TO GET EVERYTHING YOU WANT

BILL ADLER, JR.

AMACOM

AMERICAN MANAGEMENT ASSOCIATION

New York • Atlanta • Brussels • Chicago • Mexico City
San Francisco • Shanghai • Tokyo • Toronto • Washington, D.C.

This publication is designed to provide accurate and authoritative
information in regard to the subject matter covered. It is sold with
the understanding that the publisher is not engaged in rendering
legal, accounting, or other professional service. If legal advice or other
expert assistance is required, the services of a competent professional
person should be sought.

Library of Congress Cataloging-in-Publication Data

Adler, Bill
    How to negotiate like a child : unleash the little monster within to get everything you
want / Bill Adler, Jr.
        p.   cm.
    ISBN 0-8144-7294-X
    1. Negotiation in business.   2. Negotiation.   I. Title.

HD58.6.A35 2005
658.4'052—dc22   2005018460

Printing number

10   9   8   7   6   5   4   3   2   1

Contents

Acknowledgments

It goes without saying that without my daughters, Karen and Claire, this book never would have been possible—or even conceived. I won't go into details, but suffice it to say that they taught me a thing or two about negotiating, and that they were sometimes more successful than I was.

I also want to thank my wife, Peggy Robin, not only for taking over the negotiations with our children when it was apparent that I was losing, but also for her help—as always—in making sure that this manuscript was written in passable English. Ellen Kadin had the foresight to sign up my manuscript and has been a wonderful editor. Jim Bessent helped whip *How to Negotiate Like a Child* into shape. Finally, Jeanne Welsh kept all our ducks in a row while I was writing this book. Thanks everyone: I could not have done it without you.

A Note About Gender

Despite all our advances in technology, language still fails us at times. There was a "progressive" restaurant (the kind where everything on the menu was made from either soy or flaxseed) in Washington, D.C. called Food For Thought, which decided that its servers would be called "waitrons." Fortunately, the restaurant didn't exercise a strong influence on language: The term "waitron" lived and died with Food For Thought, which went out of business years ago. (That the restaurant closed its doors had nothing do to with the word *waitron,* but it did have a lot to do with the fact that you can only do so much with soy and flaxseed.)

I bring up this story because, despite Food For Thought's clunky choice of words, the restaurant's owners recognized that a gender-neutral term for "waiter" was needed so language could keep up with society. Now it's the case that a waiter can be a man or woman. But not so with "businessman," which still has strong masculine connotations.

What's a writer to do? What I've done is used "businessman," "businesswoman," and "businessperson" interchangeably, with businessman and businesswoman being used more often because they're less glaring to the mind's eye than businessperson. So my apologies in advance to any readers—and especially grammarians—whom I may have offended, insulted, upset, or affronted by my choice of words. I'm not going to try and invent "businesstron."

You're welcome.

How to Negotiate Like a Child

Introduction

Angelic. Sweet. Affectionate. These are the words that come to mind when we think of children. But there's another set of words that applies equally well to children: Stubborn. Determined. Manipulative. And winners.

The truth of the matter is that when it comes to arguing with children, children often win and the parents lose. Many parents have said to themselves, "We might as well walk all the way downstairs and get Betsy's stuffed elephant *now* because we're going to agree to do it eventually."

Children are the best negotiators in the world.

How did this state of affairs—children getting what they want and parents conceding—ever come about? How can a forty-something high-powered lawyer lose to an inexperienced four-year-old? More important, how can adults harness the astonishing negotiating prowess and skills that children have?

There's no single explanation for why children are such good negotiators. Rather, they draw on a broad range of techniques, depending on the particular situation, and including some outrageous ones that most of us have been socialized to abandon. Each of these techniques—and how you can exploit them in business and other walks of life—will be explained in detail in individual chapters.

Negotiating like a child may be the most useful and satisfying skill you can have in any aspect of life. *If you learn how to negotiate like a child, you will be able to get practically everything you want.*

Core Child-Negotiating Techniques

Here are the core techniques discussed in this book. If the list is too long to memorize, just spend time in a playground to refresh your memory.

- Throw a tantrum.

- Ask the person who's most inclined to say "yes."

- Play one side against the other.

- Get sympathy.

- Give yourself a time-out.

- Change the rules.

- Solicit a bribe.

- Move slowly and procrastinate; wear the other side down.

- Turn the negotiations into a game.

- Act irrationally.

- Worry the other side that you might be sick.

- Make weak promises.

- Win through cuteness.

- Take your toys and go home.

- Follow the rules to the letter.

- Be nice.

- Be disarmingly honest.

- Go out of your way to please the other side.

- Let the other guy think he's won.

- Stick with your gang of friends.

- Remind people that "my daddy can beat up your daddy."

You'll notice that some of these techniques involve behaving like an angel. There's nothing tough about being nice because that's the way you are. One of the things that child-negotiators prove is that being mean and nasty just because you don't care about anyone else is not going to give you an advantage. A mean personality is more likely to throw a monkey wrench into the negotiations than it is to give you an edge. (We'll go into the reasons why later on.)

The savvy reader will notice that this list can't be described with a single word or phrase such as "holistic," or "do unto others as others would do unto you," or "rules were made to be broken." The complex workings of the business world (and the world of playground politics) can't be neatly packaged as a single philosophy, technique, or school of thought. When it comes down to negotiating strategies, you need to realize what children innately know: Everybody's different. Children understand that negotiating is as much about *people* as it is about the objective. You tailor your techniques to the people around you, just as a kid might use one technique on Mom and another on Dad and yet another on a teacher or a group of friends.

Child-Negotiating Strengths and Limitations

Now to the inescapable question: What ages are we talking about here when we say "children"? For the most part, I have young kids in mind, ages two to eight. But I haven't excluded slightly younger and slightly older kids, say, from one-year-old until twelve or so. Older kids can easily revert to the negotiating strategies they were fond of just a year or so ago.

Some of the negotiating strategies I explore relate to children negotiating with other children; some involve children negotiating with adults. Which examples are which? You'll figure it out. (If you can't, then you probably shouldn't be reading this book.)

Win or lose, children move on. They get over it. Children may gloat or mope for a while, but they quickly forget—their grudges never last long. (Adults forget things, too, of course. But we tend to forget things like where the car keys are. Anything that causes angst we remember. It's the curse of being grown up.)

The techniques that children use to negotiate are often brilliant, but they sometimes lack something that's important in business: the long-range goal. Children are notorious for focusing on the here and now, and this tendency is one of the reasons they are such good negotiators. Adults think long term—which explains why they do things like develop cellular telephone networks, make advances in stem cell research, and create gourmet restaurants—though they sometimes lose sight of what they need to gain in the short term because they're too focused on a goal at the end of a long, hard road. The child's strength is the grip on the present. When a child says, "I want it *now!*" it's no use discussing the long-term benefits of waiting patiently. The truly successful child-negotiator comes away with both the immediate desire fulfilled and the long-term goal met, because the more mature party in the negotiations is forced into the position of looking at the big picture.

That's a key point to keep in mind when employing these child-negotiating techniques. You will be working from a narrow focus on the here and now. Because of that limitation, you probably won't be able to use these techniques in support of the creation of anything substantial—a cure for AIDS, a skyscraper, or a musical masterpiece. You must depend on the other party to supply the vision, or else you must supplement these child-negotiating techniques with some adult-inspired forethought and long-range thinking. Because you are *not* really a child, you can adapt, improvise, and vary your responses as required by changing circumstances. *How to Negotiate Like a Child* will provide you with some potent tools that you, as a thinking adult, will be able to use more artfully than the children who use them unthinkingly to get what they want.

There's another important point that I need to make about using these techniques: You can't use them in a halfhearted way. If you're going to throw a tantrum or appeal with cuteness, your negotiating position will be significantly diminished, to say the least, if you lose it and then say, "Only kidding." For these techniques to work, you must appear sincere in your behavior. Your performance has to be credible; otherwise, those sitting opposite you at the negotiating table may perceive you to be simply *acting* like a child.

Tapping into the Riches of Your Childhood Experience— in Business and in Life

The *How to Negotiate Like a Child* techniques can, and should, be used not only in formal business-to-business negotiations, but in every aspect of your business life. When it comes to winning, half of the battle is matching the right technique to the right players in the right situation. In this book you'll find information both on how to choose and how to carry off the techniques that could be winners for you. Timing is another key issue. Business negotiations happen every day throughout the day, and while not everything is subject to negotiations, many things are. If somebody else sees it as a negotiation, then it is one.

Who says that you should act like an adult? Who says that behaving like a child (but also knowing when that won't work) isn't the adult thing to do? We do know that in the company of other adults, especially during business negotiations, we tend to behave like everyone else around us: serious, somber, even severe. We get locked into a conformist mode and become afraid to stand out. We're afraid of embarrassing ourselves and seeming immature or unbecoming. Yet this artificial division between childhood and adulthood is just that: artificial. We're foolish to think that once we turn thirty we become adults and then, suddenly, we can no longer draw on our childhood experiences anymore. Our adult personalities and behaviors have been shaped by our childhood experiences, whether we acknowledge it or not. What I'm suggesting is that we delve deeper into our childhood and make conscious use of what we learned and did during our childhood—not shut ourselves off from our younger selves. Unlike caterpillars and other insects that truly metamorphose from one physical form into another totally different one, human children and adults are not all that different. The journey from childhood to adulthood is a continuum, and it's a great waste that so many of us discard rather than make good use of the willfulness, playfulness, and inventiveness we used every day in childhood.

Our society pushes us to hold on to youth, especially when it concerns our looks. We're obsessed with looking young, which is why cosmetic surgery is such big business. It's why we spend hours and thousands of dollars at the gym. But plastic surgery and exercise can only go so far—these are very limited tools when it comes to preserving our youth. They do little to rejuvenate our minds. What good is it to have a youthful-looking body if that body contains a cranky old mind whose idea of fun is a round of golf? Want to be youthful? Act like a child. Want to succeed in business? Use your childhood skills to break out of the constraints the adult world has built up around you. With the techniques in *How to Negotiate Like a Child*, you will regain your ability to color outside the lines.

Let me give you another perspective on the use of childhood experiences. I'm a pilot. In many ways, flying airplanes mirrors life.* Flying an airplane is a complex task, where the consequences of error are rather unforgiving. When training for a pilot's license, and throughout your aviation career, you're taught to make use of all available resources and information. In fact, that mantra—to make use of all available information—is mandated into the Federal Air Regulations. And indeed, pilots who do live long lives.

So why don't we apply this same standard in other areas of our lives, especially business? Perhaps it's because we *think* we're gleaning all available information and using all available resources when we read business intelligence reports, conduct interviews, and analyze markets. But we're not. We're not developing our most valuable resource: ourselves. It's foolish to spend so much effort and money and review on outside sources and not develop our own resources by tapping into the riches of our own childhood.

Let me mention something very important about using these techniques. No, it's not that your hands will become lethal weapons and you'll have to register them. It's not that not all of these tech-

---

* If you're interested in becoming a pilot, start with the Aircraft Owners and Pilots Association (www.aopa.org). I'm not suggesting that if you become a pilot, you're going to have a definitive edge in business, but you'll certainly develop skills that will help you in business. Among other things, pilots are able to focus during a crisis. And having a pilot's license often means that you don't have to check into the airport two hours ahead of time: You fly when you're ready to go.

niques are good for all kinds of negotiations. The techniques in this book apply—or don't—to a wide range of ways in which you might negotiate. Negotiations aren't just business-to-business dialogues; throughout the day we participate in a wide variety of negotiations, everything from getting the last doughnut in the box near the water cooler to angling for a promotion. There are many different situations where you may want to negotiate like a child, such as when you're:

- Asking for a raise

- Angling for a corner office

- Asking for some other benefit, such as a telecommuting arrangement or more comp time

- Assuming more responsibility

- Relinquishing some of your responsibilities, such as supervision of a junior staffer

- Aiming to hire an extra assistant

- Seeking management approval of your ideas for less paperwork

- Requesting a better hotel room (or at least one that's not near the ice maker)

- Trying to get a reservation at a hot, new restaurant

- Asking your company to pay for a business-class, rather than coach, ticket

- Asking for better customer service (e.g., so you don't have to wait an hour at the pharmacy for a prescription)

- Trying to get tech support to stick with you on the phone until your problem is solved

- Deciding on the details for the office holiday party

- Asking for the time off you need, either for child care or to deal with a crisis

- Determining what kind of software the company's computers should use

- Requesting a transfer to another city, of your choice

- Trying to get your moving expenses paid

- Pawning the more boring assignment off on somebody else

I mention these examples to point out that your business day is filled with myriad negotiations. If you don't think of something as a negotiation—and especially if the other side does—*you will lose*. I'm certainly not suggesting that you need to negotiate over every little thing or even most things on a daily basis. What I want you to recognize is that there are many points in the day when you're involved in a negotiation and you don't realize it. If somebody else realizes that a particular activity is actually competitive and you don't, that person may be able to take advantage of you and win. Any given competition or negotiation may be worthwhile or not worth fighting over, but it's important to recognize them as competitive activities so that you have a choice of negotiating or not. The first step in winning a negotiation is to recognize that somebody is negotiating with you.

Now let's get to some of the ways you can use the child within you to give yourself an edge.

Throw a Tantrum

The tantrum is the child's most basic negotiating skill. Nobody likes to be around somebody who's in a fit of rage, beyond reason. Our natural inclination is to flee from that person as quickly as possible. Of course, we can't always do that if the person who's having a tantrum is our daughter—or a businessperson that we have no choice but to deal with. Instead, we often give in to the demands of the tantrum thrower, especially if it's a "little thing." You can tell when that capitulation is on its way because it is often preceded by an inaudible (or even sometimes loud) sigh. We rationalize our surrender, thinking that "we're not going to lower ourselves to that level and start screaming, too." And we're right—we look superior, at least to ourselves. We're not the ones performing embarrassing antics. But look at the outcome. The calm person feels as if he is the better businessperson, but the tantrum thrower has walked away with the prize. The tantrum thrower knows that, too, which is what makes this such a powerful bargaining technique: Most of us don't want to be seen throwing tantrums, and so we concede rather than scream, shout, and stomp our feet.

The truth is that the loudest screamers and stompers often get what they want. Just think of Michael Eisner at The Walt Disney Company, or Bill Gates of Microsoft—both legendary for their tantrums. And for getting what they want.

Also, look at Larry Ellison of Oracle Corp., another CEO who is reputed to be extremely childish in the way he conducts his business: petulant, bent on revenge against anyone who's crossed him, spending company funds flagrantly on himself. Of course, you don't want to be known for throwing tantrums to benefit only yourself. You learn to use the technique to push for positive things for your company. You dig in your heels and don't budge when it's a matter of such importance that you really can't give in without abandoning your own principles. You never scream just to scream. You need to use the techniques of a child without forgetting that you're a responsible adult. You always know what the stakes are before you take this course of action. Because once you've made something into a tantrum-throwing issue, you can't back down.

Also, keep in mind that throwing a tantrum doesn't have to involve screaming. In fact, sometimes it's better to throw a quiet tantrum because nobody will know about it other than the person you're "screaming" at. Quiet tantrums usually manifest themselves in ways that are hard to describe, but you know it when you see it: All of a sudden, your mail is misdelivered. IT doesn't respond to your urgent pleas for help. On your next business trip, you find yourself in the middle seat in coach between two former winners of the Twinkie-eating competition. The person who hears the quiet tantrum runs the risk of not being believed if he tells others about it—and that gives the tantrum an extra edge, especially if you're known as a quiet, "normal" kind of person and you use the tantrum very sparingly; nobody will be the wiser.

Throwing a tantrum is a classic way in which business executives negotiate (behave, actually) like children. It can be incredibly powerful. But throwing a tantrum is effective in the same way that nuclear weapons are effective: You can't use them all that often or you will have nobody left to negotiate with.

When we read about business executives who act like children we almost always read about them in the context of throwing tantrums. Throwing a tantrum is the way that men and women revert to their childhood negotiating days. But there's no subtlety in throwing a tantrum. There's often no strategy, no creativity in it, either; no plan of attack. In that case, throwing a tantrum isn't a brilliant move; it's a tool of desperation.

I realize that these comments sound like I'm knocking the very thesis of this book, which is that you can advance your position by negotiating like a child. You certainly can. But what you can't do is use a single technique—especially throwing a tantrum—all the time. If you overuse this ploy, several bad things are bound to happen to you:

- Nobody will want to have lunch with you.

- You'll run a business (or have relationships) based on fear rather than respect.

- You'll mostly be known for your bad temper. (In the adult world, throwing a tantrum and having a bad temper are synonymous.)

- Somebody's going to slap you down one day.

But if you're known for being levelheaded, then that one time you throw a tantrum, you *will* get what you want. Throwing a tantrum is like using a very, very powerful secret weapon or a dangerous but potentially life-saving drug. Observe this rule: Use it only when nothing else will do. There's always a chance that you may never throw a tantrum in your business career, and that's okay.

Children who constantly throw tantrums are more often ignored than anything else. At home they may get spanked, sent to their rooms, or put on Ritalin. At school they get sent to the corner, or their parents are called in and told they have a problem child. They may even be asked to leave the school. Most people—parents, business colleagues, teachers—will only be moved by a tantrum from a child who's never thrown one before. Then they're stunned and are not sure how to react. Once the child has a reputation as a "tantrumer," the strategy loses its effectiveness. People shrug and say, "Oh, he does that all the time." You can be pretty sure—no, make that *absolutely* certain—that if you're the kind of businessman who's known for throwing tantrums, others will be plotting against you or will try to avoid you. It's hard to send a colleague or somebody from another company to their room as parents do with tantrumers, but the business equivalent is to fire someone. Even if you're having your first and only tantrum, you have to consider the risks. A tantrum works best not only when you have absolute confidence that your way is the only way, but also when you're sure that you are an indispensable part of the solution. Then you can be as stubborn and intractable as you like. That's the main reason it works for CEOs. They're already at the top. If they throw a tantrum and don't get what they want, the people who lose their jobs are the ones who failed to please *them*. If you have any doubts about your position, then please, please, use one of the other strategies in this book. When used under the wrong circumstances the tantrum can blow up in your face.

I've made throwing a tantrum the first and longest chapter of *How to Negotiate Like a Child* because it's the trickiest and riskiest technique, but it's also the first thing that comes to mind when we think of children's demands. Despite the notion that children are inquisitive, playful, angelic, and loving—and they are—they're also little monsters now and then. Throwing tantrums is universal among children.

Tantrums sometimes work best in group settings. In a one-on-one environment they're, well, scary. There's a fine line between people thinking you're a tantrum thrower and people thinking you're in serious need of therapy. In a room full of people you're not scaring any one individual, so the fear factor is diluted. In an enclosed office you can be pretty sure that your tantrum, directed at one individual, is going to elicit a range of conscious, subconscious, and probably primeval thoughts mostly centering around one impulse: "Get me out of here!"

There may appear to be a contradiction between this idea that tantrums work best in groups and that "quiet tantrums" also are effective. Both techniques are effective for one single, simple reason that's important to keep in mind: People are conflicted. None of us behaves in exactly the same way in the same situation, because there is no such thing as "the same situation." Seemingly contradictory approaches to dealing with business are inevitable. Likewise, kids are a fountain of contradictions and paradoxes. That's one of the reasons they are such successful negotiators: You don't know what's coming next.

You might think that from the perspective of your reputation it's better to reserve your tantrum for a one-on-one setting, lest you develop a reputation for being a loose cannon. And that's true if, as I just mentioned, you've demonstrated that you will blow up over any number of trivial incidents. But that doesn't mean that being known as a tantrum thrower over matters of genuine consequence is without its advantages. If your personality lends itself to having a temper, then there's probably nothing you can do to change your personality and you might as well take advantage of it. In that case, don't just be known as a tantrum thrower; rather, use your tantrums to generate a little fear where it really matters. Let it become known that if anyone screws up in a way that affects the integrity or structure of your company, they need to fear your wrath. Let it be known that after the tantrum comes the measured consequences. You may seem out of control during the tantrum because you don't suppress your anger. But when the tantrum is over, you assess the situation calmly and do whatever needs to be done.

Defending Against Another's Tantrums

Understanding how and why tantrums can be effective—or ineffective—can also help to defend you against somebody else who's throwing a tantrum your way. In the adult world, tantrums may indicate a personality trait (or flaw?) rather than a calculated negotiating technique. Some adults never shed this childhood behavior. But in any case, you should not let your opponent defeat you by trying to make you think that his tantrums can't be overcome; that he's going to throw tantrums always and forever unless you capitulate.

It's never a good idea to throw a tantrum yourself in response, because that would only result in what can best be described as a *Saturday Night Live* parody. Can't you visualize business executives turning into children as they hurl insults and bad words at each other? Clearly, raising the tantrum level is not the solution for dealing with somebody who uses tantrums as a business tool. Unless, of course, you have an ample supply of throat lozenges.

There are several ways to cope with and win against somebody who uses this technique:

• *Enlist the support of others.* And not those on your side of the negotiating fence, but people who may be *loosely* allied with the tantrum thrower. Find somebody else to negotiate with. It's rare that there's only one person who can negotiate for a particular side, or that only one person in a large, complex organization has the ability to decide things of importance. (In some situations that may be true: If your boss is the tantrum thrower and you're negotiating for a raise, you're stuck. But that's the exception.)

Sometimes it's a fairly straightforward process to find somebody else to negotiate with because they're already in the room with you. Other times you have to track that person down. Because you're not going to be the only person who's aware of and suffering from these tantrums, you should be able to engage somebody else with little difficulty. There's an episode of the television series *Friends* where one of the characters, Ross, notices that one of his friends, Rachel, is dating a "screamer." Rachel never catches her boyfriend in the act of throwing a tantrum, but Ross does all the time. He tries to tell Rachel (whom he still loves, but that's another plotline), but because she never witnesses the tantrums, she doesn't believe him. Fortunately, few tantrum throwers are able to keep their problem secret. You'll know and everyone around that tantrumer will know, too.

• *Just let the tantrumer have his rants.* Kids know this trick. The sister doesn't try to stop her little brother's tantrum because she knows that he'll eventually wear himself out. So she doesn't try to muzzle the tantrum thrower or mock him. She simply goes about her business as if his little outburst is beneath her notice. This usually infuriates him even more, making him redouble his screams and attempts to get attention. Then it becomes clearer to all concerned who's an effective player and who's just hot air. So, if you're sitting in a conference, find something else to do while the tantrumer is spewing fits. Read through the conference materials. Check your e-mail on your BlackBerry if you think you can get away with it, or just smile and bide your time. Eventually he'll shut up. Often at the end of a rant, the tantrumer will be tired. You may have little difficulty negotiating with somebody else at that point.

But what about the situation in which you're one-on-one with somebody who relies on throwing tantrums? That's a more difficult pickle, but one you should be prepared for, because you're bound to encounter a tantrum thrower at least once or twice in your career. The first thing to consider is just to let the tantrumer wear himself out, which can work just as well in a one-on-one situation as in a group setting. It can even work to your advantage, since many of the people who throw tantrums view those who are able to weather the storm as having passed some sort of test of toughness of spirit.

• *Pretend the tantrum didn't happen.* Of course, you can "resist" a tantrum thrower in several ways. You can just yell. You can say no and just keep saying no, or you can nod and just go on doing what you want to do. Nor does resistance have to be obvious, or even visible. Just work on getting the results you want. If, later, the tantrum thrower challenges you, you may have to reveal that you didn't accede to her wishes. There may be consequences—or not. Sometimes a tantrum thrower doesn't even remember what her goal was, so if her goal is missed, then there's nothing lost.

At the risk of getting all Zen-like, let me suggest that you simply let the tantrum blow past you. The world is filled with strange, angry people, and you're just unlucky to be working with one. But the truth is that everyone works with people like this. Years ago, when I wrote *Outwitting Neighbors,* a book about coping with difficult or oddball neighbors, I did so with a few purposes in mind. Perhaps the most important point I wanted readers to come away with was that everybody at one time or another has a neighbor that they don't get along with or is annoyingly strange. It's a fact of life: None but a hermit is insulated from bizarre and perplexing people. So we have to learn ways to cope with them.

This may be the simplest way to deal with a tantrum. If you can let the tantrum pass by you like a hot desert wind, then it will be over quickly. Often people who use tantrums to gain a negotiation advantage don't want to dwell on them or discuss them, so ignoring the tantrum, *if you can,* should work. I say that because, in the heat of the moment, tantrums are hard to ignore. Tantrums are designed to get you to capitulate right then and there. They are designed to get the other side to quickly acquiesce, because they generally can't be sustained for an extended period of time.

• *Use whatever delaying tactics you can.* Do you have to study the question? Do you need more information? Do you have to run it by the legal department? Do you need to consult an astrologer? (That last one will throw people for a loop, but suggesting that you have to confer with your astrologer might survive scrutiny by somebody who's already acting irrationally.) Because most tantrums have only short-term impact, almost any delaying technique should work to diffuse their energy.

But what about the tantrum thrower who continues to erupt? How can you possibly cope with that? Then my earlier advice holds: You need to seek allies. You have to talk frankly with your coworkers and negotiate as a team. Tantrums may intimidate your coworkers; it's up to you to develop a coalition that can, if you'll pardon the expression, drown out the tantrum thrower. People who throw tantrums assume that they're going to silence the opposition. They can only get away with it if the other side lets them.

Try a Wild and Scary Threat

A variation on the tantrum theme is to employ a wild but scary threat. Both use extremes—tantrums involve an extreme of sound and emotion; wild threats involve a large range of consequences. You know how kids threaten to hold their breath till they drop dead. Sometimes people will give in rather than wait to see how far the kid can go. That's the tactic Donald Trump used when he wanted to build Trump Tower higher than permitted under New York City's zoning laws. He said if he didn't get the height exception that he wanted, he'd build the ugliest building that he could possibly design, and site it in a way that would overshadow the historic, low-rise Tiffany's building below. He showed the city planners a hideous design. While they may not have been sure he'd really do it, they decided not to risk it and gave in. It's the technique that Mayor Anthony Williams used to help get financing for a new baseball stadium in Washington, D.C.: He basically said that if public financing for a stadium didn't go through the city council, then there's be no baseball in the nation's capital.

This technique only works if you can scare the other side into thinking that you really would carry out your threat, as wild as it is. Like a child holding her breath, you might be called upon to hold it in till your face turns blue and you feel like your lungs are about to explode. Yes, everyone around you knows that you can't really carry the threat to its ultimate point; but on the other hand, you might actually be able to hurt yourself, and you can worry them enough to give in. The potential for harm has to be there. You need to make the other side believe that the risks of potential consequences are more awful than just giving you what you want. Highway signs that say "Speed Monitored by Aircraft" aren't that effective if drivers don't see any airplanes in the sky; signs that say "Speed Limit Enforced" and that are accompanied by police cars on the side of the road are a lot more effective in gaining compliance.

For some reason when kids say "I hate you!" to their parents, the parents often (but not always!) respond by doing something to demonstrate their kindness or love. (At least the first time they're surprised by their child's scary pronouncement.) Parents do not want to be hated by their children, and even though they know in their hearts that "I hate you" is just the child's way of acting out her feelings and she doesn't really mean it, they still are willing to bend when it comes to whatever's being negotiated. Children quickly pick up on what kind of behaviors bother their parents and learn to use those behaviors as leverage.

Wild and scary threats work best when they are unanticipated. "We're going to walk out of the negotiations" isn't a terribly surprising or effective thing to say if it comes at the end of a slow build-up. And it's possibly not believable, since it's a well-known negotiating bluff. The sign on the highway that alerts drivers to airplanes that detect speeders is generally regarded as a bluff, while the radar sign combined with the police car hidden behind the billboard at the side of the road is both effective and hard to anticipate.

Just Cry

Parents can't stand to see their kids be sad. Even more—they can't stand to see their children cry. While not all parents respond the same way (many learn to stiffen their spines early on as a way to cope with lengthy bedtime wailing), some parents can't get over feelings of guilt, remorse, and sadness when they hear their children cry without thinking of themselves as failures and bad parents.

Crying is also loud. In any public place, crying causes strangers' eyes to immediately focus on the parent-in-charge, and parents don't particularly care for that kind of attention. The louder the crying and the quieter or more enclosed the space, the more likely the parent will do whatever it takes to resolve the situation—in other words, give the crier what he wants.

You see this scene played out in movies all the time, and not only with kids, but with adults, too. In the movies, the plucky heroine is about to be taken somewhere against her will. She might be in a train station. The person who wants the woman to go with him has a gun against her back. She figures if she tries to run off, he really will shoot her. But, if she calls attention to them by pretending to be his girlfriend, acting like they're in the middle of a lovers' quarrel, and she cries and screams at him, "I know all about you and my sister! I never want to see you again," it will seem natural for her to run away crying. Having made a public spectacle out of the situation, she knows it will now be impossible for him to use the gun on her and hope to fade away into the crowd. So she wails, she shakes, she sobs, she accuses. She gets all the surrounding strangers not only to notice but to sympathize and reach out to her. Her would-be kidnapper is left with no choice but to slink away before the crowd turns on him.

Kids know they can get away with crying. But even if they didn't, it wouldn't matter because crying comes naturally to children. This technique, like throwing a tantrum, is part of their nature. It's almost as if there's an inner crier waiting to be released and all that's required is the right trigger. When children get ready to cry, it's like watching a slow-motion movie: Their muscles relax, then tighten, their face swells, the eyes get puffy, and then, like a sudden cloudburst in summer, a lot of water and sound is released. You saw it coming; you could have gotten out of the way before it started to pour and there was loud thunder and dangerous lightning. But you didn't. And now that the storm has started, you need to do what you can to keep dry and safe.

While analogies often fall flat, this one—the similarities between a child bawling her eyes out in public and a severe thunderstorm—is quite apt. You need to get out of the rain; you really need to keep from being hit by lightning. While crying children aren't dangerous like lightning (so we think!), it's still highly desirable to get them to stop crying loudly in public places . . . before we're ejected from that place.

The human tendency to side with the crying person is something that criers learn to count on. There's a nurturing parent in most of us who wants to do whatever it takes to stop the crying. A child does not even have to be savvy about this technique: Cry a bit, especially in a public place, and the parent-in-charge is going to start promising or giving things to get the child to stop. After doing this two or three times, kids quickly pick up on how effective crying is.

For grown-ups, the hard part about using this technique is that no adult wants to cry in a public place. Fortunately, most adults can't bear to see another adult cry, even in a private setting. An adult always thinks that he is at least partly the cause of the other person's crying, and nobody wants to think of themselves as having failed in human-to-human interactions. When you cry, the person with whom you are negotiating will have to break stride and deal with your crying. There's simply no way they can continue the conversation or what they were doing. The tone and substance of the negotiations will no longer be under the control of that individual; *you* will be in charge. I know that it's odd to think of this technique this way. After all, you are the one who's emotionally distraught; you're the one who appears weak. And in fact, if your crying is genuine, you are going to have a difficult time making use of this technique because you *will* be distraught, not to mention sobbing. Not only are you possibly upset, but your crying may start without any advance preparation or warning. That's why I'm advising you to think about it now!

This technique—crying—is something that you may have no choice about using. But if you anticipate that you might become emotional when you go into a negotiating session, you should also be able to work through in advance what the likely responses to your crying might be, and then choose the most effective ways to respond in turn. I'm not saying that you should plan to stop crying at a certain point. If you tend to get emotional, you're unlikely to be able to turn the tears on and off just like that. I'm simply saying that if you think you might need to cry, you might want to make sure that the tears are seen by the people most likely to be moved by them. And if you think that someone will react harshly, it's also a plus if you can arrange for more sympathetic types to see that your tears were met cruelly by your adversary. You can't help but paint yourself as the victim of an overbearing and insensitive lout, making the other person come off as a bully in the process.

Of course, this technique draws heavily on all the players fitting certain stereotypes. You can't pull off the "I'm a put upon little flower" routine if you're six foot three and an ex-marine. Also keep in mind that once you play the easily wounded part, you may end up stuck with that label for a long time to come—and it could come back to hurt you when you believe you are ready to take on a leadership position. Real leaders seldom cry.

They do, however, grow into their positions. So if you've had a crying episode when you were young and starting out and you were up against someone so cruel that he reduced you to tears, don't feel you've blown any chance of ever being taken seriously again. Look for opportunities to show that you've learned from the experience. You can remind people about how you once took things too much to heart because you cared so deeply about whatever you were fighting for. People don't fault the young for that. Crying past, say, age twenty-seven or twenty-eight becomes harder to defend.

Now, let's say you're young enough and new enough at a job to be allowed to indulge your emotions with a flood of tears, if properly provoked. This, of course, raises the question: Should you pretend to cry to gain an advantage over the person you're negotiating with? In part that's an ethical question, and to the extent that you are pretending, the answer should be no. Making your sincere, spontaneous sorrow work for you is one thing; deliberately manipulating somebody is another. But what if you're on the verge of crying? Should you tap into your mental storehouse of sad images to help you start crying? My answer has to be no. Tears, like tantrums, lose their power with overuse. You're much better off learning to hold the tears back so that they come out only when you really, really can't hold them back. Because you are an adult and not a child, people don't expect you to cry easily. They're only shaken and sympathetic if you do so on rare occasions. Do so frequently, and you become the dreaded term that even very young children hate to be called: a crybaby.

It's fine to let your feelings out, but it's not good to fling them at people every time you feel slightly aggrieved. Just as you should restrain unbridled anger when it's not appropriate, you should restrain your tears when they're not truly unstoppable. Cry once too often and you will get a reputation for shedding crocodile tears. And that may lead to a party of crocodile hunters out to get you.

Pretend You Don't Hear or Understand What the Other Side Is Saying

This is one of the most ancient, yet least known, child-negotiating techniques. Children apply this technique in one of two ways: They pretend either not to understand or not to hear. In escalating tones, the child says:

"What? *What?* WHAT!?"

Eventually, the other kids give up trying to argue for what they want. In frustration, they accept the fact that the child just doesn't get it.

So the child who seemingly is oblivious to the other side's point of view ends up able to continue to arrange the dollhouse her way, or use all the Tinkertoys, or finish thumbing through *Pat the Bunny*. If you don't know what the other kid wants you to do, then you don't have to stop doing what you're doing. Parents are often the victims of this ploy: We say something to our children and get back a response that's a complete non sequitur, then we wonder, "Did Sally not hear a word I said?" Maybe. It's more likely that Sally heard everything you said—after all, she's only three feet away.

But Sally appeared not to know what to do with your statement. That's not the same as deliberately ignoring you, which she knows would make you mad. Children can get away with pretending not to hear you because they're not yet socialized to respond to every verbal query. Adults feel compelled to answer or at least acknowledge when somebody addresses them (that's how Colin Farrell got in trouble in the movie *Phone Booth*); few grown-ups have the ability to just ignore or walk away from somebody they don't want to talk to. Perhaps it's because children are often naturally shy, or because they're not yet secure in their verbal skills, or maybe it's a lot simpler than that: Kids just don't feel that they need to talk to anyone if they don't want to.

What a great skill to have. Just think how powerful you'd feel if you could just blank out on somebody entirely because you don't want to deal with them. Take telemarketers and door-to-door solicitors: We usually engage in some kind of perfunctory conversation, and that's what the telemarketer counts on. Once the conversation—the negotiation—has started, it has to come to some kind of resolution: You might buy what the telemarketer is selling or you might not. The minute you recognize that you're talking to someone who wants to disrupt your day by selling you something you don't want or need, you should immediately disengage by responding with a non sequitur or simply not responding at all. Then you'll have shut out any possibility that this particular negotiation will conclude in the telemarketer's favor.

My favorite response when a telemarketer calls is, "I don't believe you." That's one no telemarketer has ever had a response to. What can they say? "Yes, yes, I'm trying to sell you something! I'm for real!" This is a response of the "I can't hear you" type.

It always amazes me that in movies, the hero is put in a position where he has to negotiate with the bad guy. The situation always runs something like this: The bad guy has wired some priceless thing (the Declaration of Independence, the Washington Monument, Mount Rushmore—it seldom matters what it is) to blow up unless he gets the President on the line to agree to his demands. Wielding a walkie-talkie, the bad guy starts dictating the various things that the President must do to prevent the explosion. Of course, in the movie, the President seemingly plays along while hatching some clever plot of his own to trick the bad guy into blowing himself up at the very moment he thinks that the last of his demands has been met. But it seems to me that the whole mess could easily have been avoided if the bad guy couldn't get through to the President in the first place. If the President hadn't agreed to pick up the walkie-talkie, he would never have had to invent all the stalling techniques and plot turnarounds that take up the next ninety minutes of the movie. What's the lesson? Don't watch predictable potboiler movies. In addition, from the moment you think that you're going to be at a significant disadvantage in a negotiation, end the negotiation. Stop *listening*. It's not your talking that's the problem; it's that you are listening to the other side's demands. That is the source of your negotiating weakness. People have a hard time hanging up the phone, cutting off the negotiation, or closing their office door. We think we'll be perceived as rude, disrespectful, or offensive. But in fact sometimes not hearing what the other side wants you to know can give you a great advantage in negotiations. Anyone familiar with radio icon Don Imus has probably heard him use some variation of this technique on his show.

Obviously, you can't use this strategy in all circumstances: Avoidance can get you fired or result in your never making a deal that you might really need to make. But this technique is ideally suited to those situations when you have a general sense of how badly things can go for you. Some people shouldn't even get that first foot in the door, and if you slam the door even before that foot has a chance to cross your doorway, you'll be much better off.

If you are going to "pretend not to hear" someone, it's extremely important to employ this technique from the get-go. The other side can understand if you are hard to reach—e-mail sometimes fails, people go on vacation, and so on. But once they've made contact with you, and they know that you know that they want something you'd rather not give, then your "pretending not to hear" becomes transparent and it may only make them redouble their efforts to get through to you.

Let technology come to the rescue. If you have a smart cell phone, consider getting a program that tells your phone not to answer calls from certain numbers. Download a program that lets you bounce e-mail so it appears that your e-mail address isn't working (such programs actually exist). Filter e-mail from people you don't want to hear from; if you actually never see that e-mail, there's no temptation to answer it. Get caller ID and train everyone in your house to use it (your home is not a sanctuary when somebody is trying to contact you). Do whatever it takes.

Let's get back to the way kids act. Children know that if you tell them to clean up their rooms, chances are they'll have to stop playing and start straightening up, maybe not immediately, but sooner or later. But if you're not heard—or if your son thinks that you think he didn't hear—then the cleaning clock hasn't begun ticking. From children to military officers, the response is the same: If you don't hear an order you don't have to follow that order. That's why people use return receipt requested on mail, sometimes even e-mail, too: Everyone involved in any negotiation or communication knows that it's a prerequisite that there be communication between the negotiating parties before one side can gain anything.

Children hope that through this technique they can avoid the inevitable. And sometimes they can. Children know that in a war of nerves, the adults may be the first to tire. Whatever it is parents wanted their kid to do, they may discover it's easier to do it themselves. It's uncanny how some children can figure out just how long they can try a parent's patience with the "I never heard you" routine.

Even when this negotiating technique doesn't result in the unpleasant task going away (incidentally, it never works for things like "Get dressed; we're going to the doctor"), it will work to delay some tasks for children until they're ready. So, by using this technique, children are often allowed to straighten up their rooms on their own terms, to their own level of cleanliness, not yours. Why interrupt having fun with your imaginary friend if you don't have to?

Timing is often a critical element in negotiations, and the side that's in charge of them has the strongest hand. How important can timing be? Let's say that you're involved in an important (aren't they all?) negotiation on the other side's home turf. You've booked your hotel reservation for a set number of days, and you've also booked your return flight. If the other side knows that (and they most certainly do) and they can delay the meat of the negotiations until it's just about time for you to leave, then you're left with two bad choices: Leave without concluding the deal or negotiate something that's not necessarily your best deal. That's how critical timing can be.

Most negotiations are not conducted in the vacuum of a conference room. There is almost always more than a simple trade or partnership. Often one side has to obtain financing to make the negotiations work, or has to get the approval of a reluctant board, or has to win the okay of the government before making the negotiations succeed. In other words, they have to jump through several hoops. This, too, comes down to timing. You can't agree to the deal until you've secured that $10 million from the bank or you're certain that key board members will give their consent. Control the timeline for the "hoops jumping" and you control the outcome.

The main problem with delaying tactics that hinge on your not hearing or understanding is that it might be hard to pull it off with sufficient subtlety during a business negotiation. You just can't be blatant about it. That is to say, in business, you can't get away with screaming "What, what, what!?" or pretending that you don't understand your negotiating partner's Southern accent. (You might be able to get away with feigning an incomprehension of California-speak, but I leave that up to you.) Also not-so-subtle are the other business variations on this theme: not returning calls or e-mails (which tends to annoy the other side and brings out A-type personalities in even the most serene individuals). But there are clever techniques you can adopt that build on this very creative negotiating tactic.

The businessperson's version of "What, what what!?" or not hearing is to ask for more clarification from the other side. You need to see some examples, or you want to tour the other company's factory and meet some frontline workers . . . you get the idea.

So while your basic strategy is a childish wish to avoid or put off difficult negotiations, or at least slow them down so that you can use the time pressure to your own advantage, you must overlay this behavior with an adult's control over technology (when it comes to making yourself hard to reach by e-mail or by telephone), an adult's sense of what's reasonable (so that your delaying tactics never come across as too blatant), and enough subtlety to avoid giving offense where none is intended. Keep your negotiating goal in mind so that you're not simply being obstructive and unreachable as an end in itself.

A few pointers and reminders about how to apply this negotiating technique:

• *Use it selectively.* Pretending not to hear is ideally suited to dealing with people you're never going to have to work with again.

Inside your own company, it could leave you with a reputation for not listening or being too obtuse to understand a problem. Never being available to an outside party is fine, provided you're sure that the outside party really has nothing to offer you and would just be wasting your time.

• *Make gaining control of timing your goal.* Pretending you don't understand what the other side wants or is saying also works well as a means to postpone negotiations until you're ready. In that case the purpose is to control the timing to your benefit. This isn't a negotiating technique that you can always use, but it's something that if used well, with necessary subtlety, can reap tremendous benefits.

• *Use it to turn the tables on your negotiating opponent (including your boss).* Pretending not to hear or understand is one way to prevent your boss from overloading you with work that you can't do alone or might not be able to do to the standard required. Here's how that works: Your boss hands you an assignment that you know you don't have the time or resources to carry out. Instead of objecting immediately and saying that the assignment is unfair, you ask for clarification of each part of the assignment. The boss tries to explain. You ask her to go over every aspect of the task and how it should be performed. The boss elaborates, and in the process she's forced to spell out the time demands of the job, which go well beyond the normal scope of your job description. You still make it sound as if the mission hasn't been explained enough for you to know exactly what you are to do. Your boss is left with the nagging doubt the she's made a muddle of the assignment by not explaining it well enough. She is now primed to accept the fact that you might not be able to carry out the assignment as proposed, and that it wouldn't be your fault. How can you complete the work if the boss can't make clear what she wants? The boss may be forced to reevaluate the assignment, or else provide you with the resources you need, including extra time. Your boss may also have to help you meet the deadlines, or perhaps assign an assistant to you who will share the burdens. If she doesn't, and the assignment turns out badly, then it's not your fault. You've laid the groundwork for the boss to have to accept responsibility for the debacle.

After all, it was her job to communicate the mission to the person carrying out her orders. By asking questions and demanding clarification, you made clear that the assignment was problematic from the outset. It's the job of the person who sets the task to make sure that the task is clear. Pilots are required to read back clearances to air traffic control before taking off. Unless you hear the controller say "Read back correct," you may not move the airplane, you may not pass Go and collect $200. (If you do, it's going to cost you a lot more than $200, since the FAA will likely yank your pilot's license for a while.)

When you are in the boss's position, you can turn things around to your advantage if you take a few extra steps to make sure that everyone knows you explained the instructions clearly. You can even go as far as having a written memo signed by the person who's pretending not to understand. Just make sure that any neutral observers will agree that you took great effort to make things perfectly clear.

Pretend You Don't Understand to Get the Other Side to Offer Something They Didn't Plan on Conceding

Let's take the technique described in the preceding chapter to the next level. Using selective understanding to delay negotiations has its uses, but getting the other side to offer something that they didn't plan on mentioning is even better. And once somebody has offered something extra, it's hard to take that back.

Journalists do this all the time: They ask their victim . . . er, subject . . . a question or two and then stop asking questions. With the camera rolling or the microphone recording, the person being interviewed is virtually compelled to talk—actually babble. And often when confronted by silence, the babbler will say something that she didn't plan on saying. The reporter doesn't care about the silence being recorded because the reporter knows that those blank moments can be edited out (and the subject should know this, too, but usually doesn't). Nobody wants to be seen on national television looking stupid, so they talk.

Kids aren't as sophisticated; they don't realize that adults want to fill the vacuum. Kids don't self-consciously apply this technique because they aren't fazed by awkward silences as are adults. In fact, if you observe children, as I did while researching this book, you'll notice that kids are content to sit with their friends and not say anything at all for periods of time that would drive an adult to reveal all manner of personal information. It's not a problem for them or for kid-to-kid negotiations. In other words, children are immune to this negotiating tactic. However, it works well against adults. Children may not be insightful enough to realize what they're doing, but they certainly do use this tactic—and it works. The silence that they sometimes leave in answer to an adult's question prompts the adult to fill in the blank space with some new or extra promise. Adults don't know what children are thinking or plotting when they are silent (though usually kids aren't thinking about anything significant). Because of this uncertainty, which is entirely in the minds of the adults, we offer things we hadn't planned on giving.

Here's a for instance: You want your four-year-old to clean her room. It's a reasonable thing to request. But you know that your daughter doesn't want to clean her room—what kid does? (What you don't know is that your daughter also doesn't see her room as being messy and thus doesn't really understand your request at all!) At first your daughter argues with you, insisting that she needs to complete the game she is playing with her teddy bears: She can't leave them without plotting out their entire lives. For every argument you have in support of your view that she should straighten up her room, your daughter has a counterargument, until finally she runs out of things to say in response. She becomes silent and plays with her bears, despite the fact that you're not done explaining, arguing, demanding. What do you do when you're confronted with silence? You offer to buy her another bear for her family if she cleans her room! Your daughter agrees and you go away satisfied. Your daughter may or may not actually straighten up her room at that moment, even after agreeing to it, but she's going to get a new teddy bear because once you've made the offer you can't withdraw it. Or rather you can change your mind, but as every parent knows from experience, withdrawing the bear offer will cause the negotiations to collapse with little hope of recovery.

(How to get your child to clean her room is, unfortunately, beyond the scope of this book. I'm sorry.)

What should you do when you're confronted by silence? Countering this negotiating technique is very easy. All you need to do is to be aware of it—be aware of the adult tendency to avoid silence. Nature may abhor a vacuum, but people like vacuums even less. Just wait. Or meet silence with silence. Or meet silence with action. (Start taking away the bears!) Do anything but fill the silence with a promise you are sure to regret.

Share Something Important with the Other Side

Sharing a virtue, hobby, interest, spiritual perspective, background, or alma matter can be the decisive factor when it comes to negotiations, especially three-way negotiations in which you are courting, or being courted by, two other organizations or individuals.

There's almost nothing that compares to sharing something special with somebody else. We've all experienced this: You meet somebody and then, after some conversation, you discover that the two of you went to the same elementary school, share the same, rarified taste in music, stayed at the same hotel in Madrid, or enjoy a passion for mountain biking. The more exotic the connection or the more significant the shared experience, the stronger and more lasting the bond. I know that when I meet another pilot, there's an instant relationship. We share something that was very difficult to achieve and brings us a lot of happiness. I know that in a room of fifty people, if there's one other pilot, that's the person I'm going to connect to.

From their first moments as social creatures, kids immediately start to figure out what, if anything, they have in common with other kids. Then they learn that they both play with Matchbox cars or American Girl dolls; or maybe they share a fascination with *The Phantom Tollbooth,* like playing Frisbee, or delight in chocolate cake. Or maybe they both have pet rabbits. Or even just the same first name. Their passions are as strong as those of adults, and when children make a connection that involves something that they like, this connection drives their relationship, sometimes to the exclusion of other children. The circle of friends is narrowed to those kids who share whatever it is that fascinates them. This glue is easy to underestimate, especially since children often forget why it is that they developed such a solid relationship.

As with many things that kids do, the adult way is a little more complex and has some pitfalls. But first, another few words about how to make use of this strategy. It pays to research the hobbies of your negotiating partners. Find out what they like. Even if you don't share all the same interests, there probably will be some over-lap of experiences in any group you might assemble at random, so you'll have something to talk about other than business. If your boss or new office mates like competitive chess, well, then the more you know about chess the more you'll be able to talk about it and consequently improve your relationship.

It's especially helpful to get to know something about your negotiating counterpart's special interests when he's into something obscure or esoteric. If he plays golf, he'll easily have potential business partners inviting him to the links on a nice day. You can be one of those extending an invitation, and you won't stand out. But what if you learn that in addition to golf, he's also an expert on butterfly migration. Do a little research of your own on the subject and then ask some intelligent questions; perhaps even suggest a visit to a traveling butterfly exhibit when it comes to town. I would bet he'll be delighted to find someone with an interest in his hobby, and that common ground could well become the basis for a friendship that solidifies the relationship that began as purely business. And you might find yourself with a new and fascinating hobby as a side benefit.

The more links you have between you and the person with whom you're negotiating, the greater the chance that something positive will result. And these connections will give you a stronger relationship than others who are involved in the negotiations may have.

Sharing something in common with the other side is more of a broad strategic measure than a negotiating tactic. This is something you should *always* do when you encounter new people who you need to deal with on several levels: Develop some kind of personal bond or relationship that goes beyond the give-and-take of negotiations. That way, they won't view you simply as someone who wants to get something from them, someone they deal with only because they must. They will view you as a whole person, and you will see them more completely, too.

But—and here's that warning—whenever a business relationship develops into a personal relationship there's the risk of a falling out, as can happen when people jump to the conclusion that they've got a lot of things in common and then, over time, discover a conflict over this or that particular issue. Unlike children, who sometimes rush to declare someone their new best friend, only to feud, declare the person an enemy for a short time, and then make up, adult friendships are far less flexible. Because you will need to continue to work alongside certain people for business, you will always need to keep a certain businesslike detachment. You can share interests—even passions—but keep yourself from going overboard.

Remember, Martha Stewart thought she had a close friendship with her stockbroker, and she thought that friendship meant that she was entitled to insider information about the stock she owned. She even remarked to another friend, "Isn't it nice to have stockbrokers who will tell you these things!" But it turned out that it wasn't that nice for either of them; they both ended up with identical sentences of five months in prison and five months of house arrest. So share your interests, share your passions, develop your relationship . . . as far as ethics, good business sense, and the law will allow.

Call in Backup (Or "My Dad Can Beat Up Your Dad")

In business, the variations on this technique may be "My lawyer can beat up your lawyer," or "My bank will give me enough capital to buy you out if you don't agree to my terms." That sort of thing.

The problem with this approach is that you'd better be willing to follow up or your reputation is toast. Kids quickly realize this: "I'm going to sic my dog, Killer, on you if you don't trade baseball bats with me." Some kids will make the trade to avoid having to look over their shoulder every time they think they hear the padding of a dog behind them. Maybe even most kids will assume that it's not a bluff. But every now and then you find a kid who won't accede to the bluff. Then the game's over. Not only does the bluff no longer work, but the bluffer's stature is forever diminished—until he gets transferred to another school, that is. Children don't often think about the consequences of their bluff being called—remember, they're focused on the present, not on what *might* happen in the future—but you need to be keenly aware of all the permutations of your bluff failing.

You can use the "My dad can beat up your dad" technique

perhaps with a little more subtlety, but if you're unwilling to follow though, your reputation will be tarnished and your negotiating position weakened. While this is true for all of the methods in this book, it's especially important that you have a realistic appraisal of your side's strength when you use this technique. You can't threaten to sic your killer dog on someone if all you've got is a lapdog. You can't threaten to wear the other side down with relentless litigation if the other side has its own gang of lawyers who have done the same to others. Children sometimes assume that their dad or their dog is the biggest, toughest, most protective being on the planet. Their fierce loyalty and belief in the idea that wishing can make something come true leads them to use this tactic in the face of countervailing reality. But for an adult to succeed by claiming a strong or fierce protector, there actually has to be one.

Of course, the big, tough protector doesn't have to be at your beck and call. It may be enough that the protector you call upon has an intimidating reputation. Just like the kid whose dad is a cop or a professional athlete, you may not need to do anything more than let your adversary know who your protector is. For example, if you receive a letter threatening you for nonpayment of an amount you know has been falsely billed to you, you may not have to call on your state's consumer affairs department to protect you from the collection agent; it's sufficient to write a letter to the company letting them know that you're aware that you have the protection of your state's consumer law and will file a complaint if the false billing does not cease.

But what if you live in a state with weak consumer protection laws? What if you don't actually have any strong force to back you up? Who can you say you'll get to defend you if no one comes to mind? This is the situation for the kid whose dad is the proverbial ninety-eight-pound weakling. Kids are stuck with the families they happen to end up with. But in the business world, you can choose your protectors, to a certain extent. You can, in effect, get a stronger "dad" before the negotiations even begin. So if your company keeps a law firm on retainer, you make sure it's a firm known for being tough and winning at all cost. If you need to project financial strength, you make sure that your company has a solid relationship with a bank or brokerage firm. Whether having a tough, resourceful partner can enhance your negotiating position depends on what you're negotiating, of course. Sometimes it's worth the effort, time, and expense to have a business "dad" who can beat up the other side's business "dad." For that, you need to know your opponent's intentions and level of aggressiveness. That is, you'll have to see if and how they flex their muscles.

Older kids flex their own muscles. That's a lot different from saying "My dad can beat up your dad." The behavior of older children—teenage boys in particular—isn't especially relevant to negotiations between businesspeople. It's the poorly disciplined, unsuccessful boys who try to get what they want by direct aggression. They may end up in detention or in juvenile court for their hostile actions, not on the boards of corporations.

Here it's the younger kid who's actually the shrewder player. He doesn't threaten to pound the other side into submission with his own might. He just tries to make the other side afraid to take his side on. So if you're planning on being tough, borrow from what younger kids do; don't emulate the older children, who may be too tough for their own good.

You should also keep in mind that you don't want to flaunt your tough protector too much. Kids may do that, but children aren't negotiating a critical business deal and the stakes aren't necessarily as high for them as they are for you. You want to create a subtle sense that you could, might, and possibly will call on an outside force. You want to use this tactic to give you an edge, perhaps the decisive edge, not to defeat the other side and cause the negotiations to fall through. Many techniques that children use are reasonably foolproof, but some have the potential to bite you back. Or, as kids would say, bite you in the backside. Use this one judiciously.

Because this strategy only works when you have really big guns (and then not all the time), the best way to counter it is to focus on the other side's weakness. Everybody, every organization has a weakness. Perhaps even more than one. My kids taught me this strategy through the board game, Sorry. In Sorry, the player who gets all her pieces at the destination first wins. But along the way you can bump other players' pieces—sending them back. (This same twist was a popular component in many board games from days gone by, including Careers, where you not only try to advance your career, but thwart your opponent's success, too.) It's important to advance your pieces along the board as quickly as possible. But when confronted with a choice of whether you should advance your own piece or create a setback for your opponent, how do you choose? How do you know what the best strategy is? The answer, my kids showed me, is quite simple: Do whatever your opponent would like least. Put yourself in your opponent's position for a moment and consider what would be the worst outcome. Once you've figured that out, then make that play.

The same strategy can work well when countering the "My daddy can beat up your daddy" situation. Do whatever the other side wants least. Take the time to figure out where the other side's weakness lies. Once you know that, you can figure out how to approach them from their weakest point. It may take some time to puzzle out the weak spot, since any organization will do its best to project an image of uniform strength. But sometimes a little poking around will reveal that on one side or the other, the walls are not as strong or as high as they appear to be.

Your best bet in that case might be to extract the concessions you want in exchange for your promise to continue to act as if your opponent is strong and did not give in. In legal terms, this means you settle your claim for an undisclosed amount and the other side never has to admit they did anything wrong. Your negotiating opponents appear not to have cracked—at least to the rest of the world—but you and only you know they've caved.

Don't Think About Negotiating—Just Do It

There are critical differences between the way you may have learned to negotiate and how children negotiate. Kids do something that's not taught in Harvard Business School (which is why this book will give you a leg up in negotiations, even if those you are up against went to Harvard). Adults plan, theorize, strategize, and agonize. They think and, quite often, they think too much. Kids just do.

There are, of course, certain advantages to thinking about the negotiations in advance. You need to understand your objectives, the other side's objectives, your limitations (financial and otherwise), how the negotiations integrate into your overall business plans, your staffing requirements, and so on. In the real world, sometimes you can't just wing it.

But kids don't have staffing requirements, long-range goals, or anything like that. Yes, that will put them at a disadvantage when it comes to integrating their needs into a five-year business plan. But that doesn't matter because children don't have any need for a five-year plan. When they negotiate, it's for something in the here and now. Kids barely have a *five-minute* plan. And that's why when it comes to negotiations over short-term issues, they're the champs. Children focus on the present; they know what they want and go for it, undistracted by ancillary missions or long-range problems. It's this amazing focus, this single-mindedness of purpose, that enables children to negotiate with a doggedness and effectiveness that few adults can match. Kids are not conflicted about doing things: They don't worry that if they do the thing that their boss wants, they might alienate their coworkers. When you have a one-year, five-year, or ten-year goal, there are going to be all sorts of complications and prioritizing. You may lose sight of what your immediate needs really are.

Adults involved in negotiations are not only distracted by business issues, but by personal ones, too. Sometime during your negotiation meeting, someone may be thinking:

"Gee, he's cute. Maybe just a little fling . . ."

"I'm tired of Oklahoma City; I just want to get back to LA."

"I should have brought a charger for my iPod."

"I can't stand another PowerPoint presentation!"

"Will Quinn try to claim my office if I'm gone any longer?"

"Wish I'd had time for a smoke before this meeting started. It's time for a cigarette break."

"What a view—maybe it's time to switch companies."

"I don't want to miss my kid's soccer game! Let's wrap this up."

These personal concerns, which percolate in the mind of everyone who's involved in negotiations, can have an impact on the way negotiations are conducted. When kids act out during long, dull meetings, no one's surprised: We all know kids will be kids. But adults are expected to be in control at all times. They're held to a higher standard, especially in the business world, where everyone tries to make a point of appearing ultra-professional at all times. Still, I'd bet the ranch that a negotiation has never transpired without these kind of thoughts taking over each person's mind for at least a part of the time.

> The reason why worry kills more people than work is that more people worry than work.
>
>   Robert Frost

You root around for a solution and may come up with an answer: Zen. Zen's the antidote. Empty your mind of everything other than the task at hand. Be one with the calm sound of central air-conditioning.

Nice try. Zen doesn't make the meeting any shorter or stop the person next to you from clicking his pen-top compulsively and fidgeting with his feet under the table. Zen doesn't postpone your son's soccer game. Zen doesn't eliminate the nagging worry that if these negotiations don't wrap up in the next ten minutes, you're going to miss your flight home and end up on the red-eye in a middle seat between two incredibly huge passengers. Zen is good for selling books on Zen, and it's good for expensive spas in Arizona, but it won't help you in the here and now. What will help you here is the sense of immediacy that children bring to their negotiations: Just do it. Speak out. Ask for what you want bluntly. Focus on what you need to accomplish and look for the most direct way to get it. Do what you can to cut through all the distractions, delaying tactics, and negotiating nuances that others are throwing your way.

Kids just speak up and say what's on their minds. That can be a breath of fresh air. It can also be indiscreet or incredibly embarrassing, depending on what's on the kid's mind. But as an adult, you have the sense to avoid saying anything stupid or hurtful, and you can figure out how to cut through the bull and get to the point of the meeting without making anyone feel offended.

But what if there's no chance for you to push things along? What if you have no say in how the negotiation meeting is run? Then it's a matter of keeping yourself awake and focused, despite all the distractions and worries that may trouble you. How? One thing that may help is to remember that your negotiating opponent has an equal—though different—number of worries. She who worries less negotiates best.

Advice that tells you not to worry or fret is one thing; actually developing the skills to practice that advice is another. I'll say this at the outset: Some people can learn not worry more easily than others. It's the sort of thing that comes naturally to certain types of personalities, while others seem born to worry over everything that can go wrong. Don't fight your nature—just find some coping techniques you can use while sitting silently in a meeting. Maybe that guy who's fidgeting with his feet under the table is onto something; it could be his method of working out his anxieties. Try out different things that help your stamina and concentration. Talk silently to yourself, perhaps. Get an internal dialogue going about whether you compartmentalize or squash some thoughts. During this process, you will think about those issues and problems you need to address and take your mind off the ones that don't matter right now.

Of course, you can never discipline your wandering thoughts perfectly. Accept the fact that no matter how "Zen" you are, a few stray bad thoughts are going to find a way back inside your brain. In that case, your job is to let them slide by. If you're the kind of person who isn't bothered by somebody yakking on a cell phone at the dinner table next to you, or by the flash of passing truck lights in your motel room, or the passenger who's humming in the seat behind you, then chances are pretty good that you will be able to put these distracting thoughts away for the duration of the negotiations.

But what if you're the kind of person who glares at the parents who are settling themselves and their one-year-old down in the row behind you on the airplane, and then spends the rest of the flight waiting for the sleeping baby to wake up and start to wail? If you find yourself constantly worrying about things that haven't happened but could happen, chances are that you're not going to be able to compartmentalize your mind or hold distracting thoughts at bay for the duration of the negotiations. If that's the case and you're a bona fide worrier, then you're not the best candidate to put the "don't think about it" strategy to use. You're going to need to look into a more adult way to prevent yourself from torturing yourself with your worst thoughts and fears. A good therapist, perhaps?

Be Nice

Does being nice run counter to the negotiating tactic that says "My dad can beat up your dad"? Sure it does. But so what? Kids don't strive for consistency; they just do whatever they think will work. Grown-ups think they need to be logical and consistent, but as Emerson observed, "A foolish consistency is the hobgoblin of little minds." Children, by their spontaneity, often have a more suitable handle on a given situation than adults, who may be too concerned with preserving an image or fulfilling a given role. But in situation-driven negotiations, it's an advantage to be flexible, to be able to act one way with one set of people and take the opposite tack with another.

So flex your "My dad can beat up your dad" muscle on alternate Tuesdays, and be nice the rest of the time. Use your adult judgment to size up the situation and the people involved—and if it seems to you that a childlike sweetness and a go-along attitude would work better than a tough-guy stance, then be as sweet and angelic as you've ever been in your life.

I'm not going to write about how being nice helps reduce your blood pressure, carries over positively into your family life, alleviates stress, helps you think more clearly and focus on your goals, and bolsters your ability to deal with people who aren't nice. What I am going to do is show you how children make use of this negotiating tactic and how you can translate that information into better business negotiations.

There are two kinds of people. (It's a standard cliché for every business book to divide people into two different groups, so I ask your forgiveness in advance.) The first group is made up of nasty, unkind, egotistical, malicious, and unpleasant jerks. The second group is made up of pleasant, kind, polite, amusing, considerate individuals. With whom would you rather spend hours or days?

The answer is the same for children as it is for businesspeople.

What do children do when they're thrown into a situation with nasty, toy-grabbing, sand-throwing meanies? The nice children may get taken advantage of on the first encounter, it's true. But they also tend to look for ways to avoid future encounters. When play dates are being proposed, the mean kids don't get asked back.

How does that translate to adult business? Repeat business and satisfied customers are the backbone of many, if not most, business transactions. If people think you've behaved like a jerk, they'll go out of their way to avoid you next time they need whatever it is you're selling. They may even prefer to pay more for a product or a service if it means avoiding doing business with someone they find inconsiderate or hard to get along with.

So play nice, and the other kids will continue to play with you. Be polite, be friendly, be sweet, and they'll tell their friends that you were a good person to deal with. It's that simple.

Despite the simplicity, this may be one of the most difficult concepts for hard-nosed businessmen and businesswomen to assimilate. After all, getting ahead in business is all about being tough, they think. Nice guys finish last, the saying goes. Well, at least that's what the people who *aren't* nice keep saying. Nice guys can finish last, but that's only if they're nice and only nice. If you combine nice with competence, imagination, and hard work, I say you've got a winning combination. Add to the mix some creativity and drive, and it's clear you'll go far, whether on the playground or in the boardroom.

Be Disarmingly Honest

It's not that kids don't ever lie. All kids at some point want to find out if they can get away with bending the truth. They experiment with lying from the time they learn to talk. "Did you eat all your broccoli?" the parent asks. "All of it," the kid says proudly, thinking that nobody was looking as he quickly transferred the serving from his plate to the floor, where the dog quickly gulped it down. But parents aren't fooled. They know he couldn't have eaten it all so quickly. They can see the telltale sauce-tracks running off the edge of the plate. They check the floor and find the bits that the dog didn't lick up. And then they let the kid know that they aren't fooled, and they make sure he learns that lying is a serious thing—something with consequences.

But there are always kids who don't learn the lesson. Either they succeed in fooling their parents, or they succeed in evading the consequences. They learn to justify their actions to themselves. They come to think of themselves as too clever to be caught. I'd like to be able to assure you that these people do badly in the business world. People learn they can't be trusted. People don't like them and avoid dealing with them if they have a choice. In a more just world, that would be the case. But I'm sorry to say, in the real world, quite often cheaters—and liars—do prosper. Still you wouldn't want your kid to be one, and you don't want to be one yourself.

I'm trusting that you don't need a lesson on the underlying immorality of lying. You know it's wrong. This book isn't about morality, it's about what kids can teach us that's of use in business negotiations. So let me come back to the broccoli story. The reason the kid is caught is because kids, when they lie, do it clumsily. They leave trails of evidence. They can't remember the previous lies they told, so they have a hard time keeping their stories straight. That's good, because it means that they get caught easily and learn that being caught brings consequences.

Adults who lie not only lack a sense of morality, they usually are also overconfident of their ability to deceive. They really think they can lie well enough to get away with it, to benefit from their deception. But most people just aren't that good at it. Sooner or later they trip up. Yes, as I've said, we have to concede that some people get away with lying their way to business success. But any habitual liar has got to worry constantly about being found out.

And what do adults do when they find out a business deal was based on a lie? They cancel the contract; they call the police and complain of fraud. And they file multimillion-dollar lawsuits. The consequences can be a whole hell of a lot worse than being deprived of dessert for a week.

Be Yourself

Kids don't adopt different personas to fit the occasion. Kids are who they are; what you see is what you get. And kids know that about each other. They know which children are shy, loud, exaggerate a lot, like to play Frisbee instead of soccer, have lots of interesting things in their pockets all the time, tell good jokes, tell bad jokes—in other words, kids have their strengths and weaknesses. You get to know a kid and you know what you're getting. Few kids can pull off passing themselves off as something they're not. And kids are usually quite good at spotting adult phonies when they see them.

In my opinion, this ability helps streamline and speed up the negotiation process because you don't have to first penetrate the other kid's persona. You don't have to try and peel away their inner motivations or desires: No onions here. You might think that this, in fact, is a bad idea; that it's a weakness to be open about who you are and what you want. But that's only if it's part of your game plan to actually hide what your negotiating goals are—a strategy that can all too easily backfire. By keeping true to yourself, you'll find that the people you are negotiating with will relax a little, too—and perhaps even let down their shields.

To the extent that you are yourself, and to the extent that people can count on you to be the person you show yourself to be, others will perceive that *you* are the reason that things went so smoothly. You'll enhance your personal reputation. In an environment where people are used to playing their cards close to the chest—indeed, an environment in which people expect diversions and subterfuge—the person who can get rid of all of that will become somebody other people want to negotiate with. If doing deals is what you do for a living, it's to your advantage to have people know you and be able to tell others who you are and what they can expect when they deal with you. You'll be like the kid who collects baseball cards, the one all the other kids want to trade with.

How do you become yourself? I can't give you step-by-step instructions, and indeed it may be a difficult thing for you to do. After all, if you're like many people in business you are used to a certain amount of aloofness and pretext. Office politics requires that you act like a politician, and all politicians distance their behavior from the way they are when they're not at the office. Perhaps the cure is to spend a little more of your free time among kids, watching them, playing with them, enjoying them for their own unique selves, and a little less time in the cubicles where adults jockey for position and the upper hand.

Know Your Own Team

The next thing you need to know are the people you depend on and who depend on you: your own team. Children learn quickly that they can often accomplish more faster if they work together. Even brothers and sisters will form alliances (albeit temporary ones) when it suits their interests. Alliances not only let individuals cooperate, they also mean that you're not working at odds with people—you don't have to divert your intellectual resources from your primary objective. But you can only form an alliance when you know what your partners want. So get to know them.

If you're a kid, that means knowing who's on your side. It may be the kids you play soccer or baseball with, or whatever sport you prefer. It could be your classmates. Or it could be just the group of kids you hang out with. For an adult, it's your colleagues, the people at your company. It may not be the whole enchilada; lots of times there's some group of people within your own company that you'll view as the competition you're up against: You're competing for office space, budget, choice assignment, or promotions. I leave it up to you to define who you will regard as "us" and "them."

Once you've decided who your teammates are and who's on the opposing side, you have to know your people and their strengths and their weaknesses. (I'll be talking a lot more later about various ways to scope out your opposition.) You get to know them just as you did your pals on the playground, by actually playing with them. That is, you want to do more than just work with them. You want to relax with them. Get your families to know their families. Find out what you have in common, and find out also the things that you don't have in common. Then you'll be able to appreciate the diversity and find the qualities and resources that others may have that you lack.

This isn't exactly unpleasant work, either. It means that you'll go out together for drinks after work, have parties either at work or on weekends (why not both?), and observe each other's birthdays and milestones. No, I don't mean with funny hats, cupcakes, and birthday presents, like you did for each birthday child when you were in kindergarten. It is important to keep these things low-key and to avoid the sense that it's compulsory to celebrate each passing year with a lot of whoop-de-do (regardless of how the birthday boy or girl feels about it). I'm merely arguing here against the opposite: the rigid separation of home-life and work-life that all too often becomes institutionalized in large corporations where lots of strangers are thrown together from nine to five. It's so much easier to achieve a stated end when you have developed a sense of comradeship with the people you're working with.

That's not to say that you must become close friends with the people on your team. There may be personality clashes; there may be many differences of opinion. But you do need to develop respect and tolerance for each other, and find ways to appreciate the differences you have. Young children aren't equipped to do this. Teamwork skills generally don't develop until the middle of childhood, seldom earlier than age nine or ten. They tend to develop earlier among boys than among girls. (Perhaps that's a relic of the past, when girls were less likely to play on teams than boys were. But these days, with the enormous popularity of girls' soccer teams, that may no longer be the case, as it surely was when I was growing up.)

Though your friendship with your work teammates will seldom be as deep and as lasting as your friendships from school or from shared interests, that's not to say it's impossible for them to be. Business friendships that arise under very stressful conditions, such as during tense and extremely high-risk negotiations, have something of the Stockholm Syndrome about them. (That's the name given to the strange sympathy and closeness that's been known to develop between hostage takers and their hostages. It is a relationship created out of a forced proximity and shared interest in an outcome. Both the prisoners and the captors may be afraid of being killed in a police raid, for instance; both the prisoners and the captors have to share the same food, cramped conditions, lack of facilities, and so on.) In the workplace, it doesn't really matter too much if you don't develop friendships that go to a deeper level. So what if there's not much going on beyond the surface. If someone on your team left the team tomorrow, would you still go out of your way to see that person? Maybe not, but that doesn't mean that you can't get all the support you need from each other while you're on the same team.

That's usually good enough for kids. They play with one team in the summer when the sport is baseball, and they get to know each other well enough to work happily enough together. And then, when it's basketball season, they go on to become part of another team of kids and get to know those kids well, and maybe that group operates with quite a different group dynamic. But kids adapt to the different team styles and learn to fit right in. When it's time for soccer, it's another group yet again, and new adjustments need to be made.

Not everyone can slide so easily in and out of different groups. Some kids never feel comfortable with the idea of team play; they're better at solo or one-on-one sports. That doesn't mean they won't be good team players in the business world. It's easy to draw analogies between the type of team play we learn as kids and the way colleagues at work learn to function as a team—just as I've done here—but let's not get too literal-minded. Here I speak as one of those boys who was always picked last for team sports. Let me add that I never let my klutzy sports past handicap me when it came to my adult business dealings (and neither should you).

Play Your Best Game

If you don't like the game that's being played, get everyone to play something else—a game in which you have greater say over the rules and the players.

Children can learn chess at a young age, but they often prefer checkers. Other kids like board games like Sorry, Parcheesi, Candy Land, or Monopoly. Why? Some kids do better with checkers because the strategy is simpler; for others, Candy Land has the excitement, the color, and the tempting subject matter. Sorry is largely a matter of luck—some kids like it best for just that reason. Monopoly involves lots of personal trades and judgment, as well as a lot of luck.

So what happens when a chess player gets together with a Sorry fan? There's a deep and protracted negotiation over which game to play. The main reason is that the chess player is clearly the intellectual type, while the Sorry player is obviously not as bright. (Only kidding.) No, the real reason is that kids like to play what they like to play—it's that simple. Given a choice between chocolate and vanilla ice cream, somebody who likes chocolate is going to choose chocolate over vanilla 999 out of 1,000 times. That's in a kid's nature, and it's something that doesn't change all that much as they grow up.

But there are consequences to a negotiation over what kind of game to play. If you're successful in getting the other side to play your game, the one you're best at, the one you enjoy, you give yourself the advantage in the game itself. Business negotiations are like that, too. If you get to choose the time and place and the types of things that are up for grabs, you're playing your best game, and you have the advantage.

That's why pre-negotiations—talks about setting up the negotiations, and the scope of the negotiations—are oftentimes as important as what goes on once you're in the thick of things. They may even be more important. Let's go back to the analogy of children choosing a board game: If the child who's a good chess player can convince the child who prefers Sorry that it will be fun to try chess, there's no question about who's going to win the chess game. On the other hand, if the child who likes playing Sorry can get the chess whiz to play a game that's virtually all luck, then they're on an even playing field, and the Sorry-preferring child at least has an even chance.

That's why children often spend as much time arguing about which board game to play as they do actually playing the game itself. They understand that the experience of playing one type of game will be vastly different from playing another. If chess ends up being the game, then the Sorry player's best bet is to enlist another chess whiz to be on his side. Or if that's not possible, he'll put off playing until he's had time to learn much more about the game. Or at the very least, he'll insist upon a relaxation of the rules: The less experienced player should be allowed more time for moves, or be allowed to take back a move that he quickly sees was a poor choice.

Adults use variations on these themes all the time: They bring in an outside expert to coach them through the unfamiliar part of a specialized business deal. They negotiate for extra time to investigate an unfamiliar situation. They write an escape clause into a contract that gives them an out if a decision turns out to have terrible consequences for their business. Along the way they learn how the other game is played. That is to say, the Sorry player, after getting plenty of expert advice and experience with chess, can actually end up being the chess whiz himself—and in that case, he may actually suggest a game of chess the next time he's the one who gets to choose which game is being played.

Learning to play new games gives people new skills and can bring other changes, too. Parents of schoolchildren see this happen all the time. At parent-teacher conferences, parents hear that their little Julie is smart, well behaved, and never lashes out at other children. "Are you talking about *my* child?" is the sometimes quizzical reply. Parents regularly get reports about children who are supposed to be their offspring, but from the description appear to be somebody else's children. How is that possible? How can a kid behave one way at home—often sarcastic, for instance—and another way at school? The answer is sometimes found in the behavior needed to succeed in team games at school. The kid who may be "mouthy" at home with his parents may be the same kid who, having found a sport that he's good at, is a disciplined, dedicated, and well-integrated part of the team. The coach tells the parents their kid is a model of cooperation and sportsmanship. Being good at something and being looked up to by others for being a leader at a game gives children confidence and often brings out the best in them.

The reason some people succeed in their chosen field, when they're not generally perceived as role models in other aspects of their lives, is that those people have become comfortable and experienced at playing a game (or rather, doing business) their way, and they've succeeded in getting others to play on their terms as well.

Be Direct About Your Needs

Ice cream. *That* stuffed bear. *That* Barbie. To be picked up. To be put down. *Not* to take a nap. A fairy tale before bedtime. When a child knows what she wants, she's relentless about getting it. If you're a parent and you don't pay attention to what your child really wants, you're going to lose the negotiation every time.

Most of the time children are completely transparent about what they want. When a child clings to a stuffed bear in a store like a mountain climber holding on to a cliff overhang, you know what she wants. She's not secretly telegraphing you a message that she really wants the stuffed alligator in the other aisle.

From the child's perspective, the negotiation is straightforward and simple. No trickery, deception, fraud, or ruses: I want this stuffed bear.

Look at the way adults behave, in contrast. Let's say your wife suggests going out to Beppo's Italian Garden for dinner. You object, saying, "I don't like the service there." But the real reason you don't want to go to Beppo's is that you have zero willpower and will be compelled to order the cannoli for dessert, with the certainty of adding an extra inch to your waist. And with that high school reunion coming up in two weeks . . . well, let's just say that you've always wanted to impress a certain someone you knew in high school fifteen years ago.

It's so complicated: All you want to do is avoid several hundred extra calories. But you don't say that. What happens next? You play a few rounds of a game, a cross between Twenty Questions and The Weakest Link, as your wife probes the depth of your deception, quizzing you on exactly what's wrong with the service at Beppo's Italian Garden. How much simpler—and more effective for you—it would have been to make your mission (reasonably) transparent: "I can't resist their cannoli and I want to keep the weight off" would probably have won the negotiation for you.

Let's get back to the way children negotiate. A child who wants to be carried because it's a sweltering August day and there's a steep hill ahead will almost certainly achieve that goal for a number of reasons (kids can, and do, combine negotiating strategies). Because you know that's all you have to concede, in your mind, it's an easy "mission accomplished"—just carry Jennifer until you're drenched with sweat and wheezing like you're in the middle of a pollen cloud and the deal's done. Uncomplicated and clear-cut. Sure, it's a lot of work and Jennifer really is old enough to walk, but she made the negotiating process easy for you by making your part understandable and easy to implement.

Clarity is an important aspect of negotiations. When the other side needs to see your cards to understand the strength of your position, you lay the cards out on the table. Hugging them close to your chest gets you nowhere.

Take Your Ball and Go Home

It's simple: You don't like the way the negotiations are going and you just take your toy and walk away. Kids don't hesitate about using this ploy. Even more strategically, while children will sometimes announce in advance, "If you don't let my little sister play, too, I'm going to take my train home," they're just as likely to pick up their possessions and walk away. That is the beauty of this negotiating technique: It can be used as a potential threat—like a tree limb that's about to fall off—or as a warning that you'd better heed or at least take into account.

Let's look at the way children employ the more subtle technique. A child who announces that he might take his basketball and go home may or may not get his way. Why? A basketball's not exactly a rare commodity. If another kid can run home and bring back a ball, then the play will continue without the kid. But if he's the only basketball owner among that group of kids, then they're going to have to let him play the game. This is really a basic principle of capitalism; Karl Marx called it "ownership of the means of production." And yet it's so simple that every child can grasp the concept at once.

What children sometimes fail to grasp, however, is that ownership brings responsibilities, too. If the owner of the ball becomes too dictatorial, ordering other players to overlook his fouls or demanding that other rules be bent unfairly in his favor, there's always the danger that the other players will revolt, grab the ball away from him, and send him home with nothing. That's an extreme case, perhaps. Another, more common risk is that the other kids will decide they don't want to play with him anymore. They'll go out and get their own ball, or find a new friend who's not so demanding. So the adult who asserts the workplace equivalent of "I'll take my ball and go home" needs to know ahead of time that another ball can't be obtained just as easily from somewhere else. And he's got to be sure that there's enough time pressure to force the other players to make a snap decision, rather than put things on hold and try to work out a solution without him.

For the adult who's confident that the game can't go on without him, this is a potent strategy. But it's also something (much like throwing a tantrum) that can only be used once or at most twice in a career, to avoid damage to one's reputation. If you let yourself become known as someone who might walk out in a huff, you may not be invited to come to the game in the first place—ball or no ball.

Stick with Your Gang

Kids pick their friends, and they're innately smart about it: From an early age they learn to avoid malcontents, jerks, and just plain unpleasant children. It isn't about choosing your negotiating opponent—this technique is a long-term negotiating tool that involves keeping in close contact with your friends, family, and other people you trust and get along with. Having this support structure helps you in myriad ways when you get into intense negotiations. Children have a small but solid support structure that consists of mommy, daddy, and close friends.

Whether they realize it or not, having a stalwart network of family and friends helps put kids on a firm footing when they negotiate with other children. There's something about knowing in the back of your mind that no matter what, somebody's going to back you up emotionally, intellectually, and in other ways. It's not a matter of running home to mommy and daddy in real life; there's an inner strength that comes from knowing that no matter what happens you're going to have the love and support of the people around you. Children learn this from experience: Loyalty is price-

less. It's a subconscious faith that changes the way children approach and participate in negotiations. The importance of having
people around you that you know you can count on can't be quan-
tified, but it also can't be overemphasized. A child who feels that
she's got nothing to look forward to at home will be weak at the
knees.

Children develop self-confidence in small increments over a
long period of time; they're born insecure. Children take—well,
pardon the pun—baby steps toward being poised and assured; and
these steps are helped by knowing that mommy and daddy will be
there for them.

The same is true for adults involved in business negotiations.
An adult who is new to a town and has not yet made friends and is
far from his family will almost always be at a disadvantage when up
against an adversary who is in a familiar setting, surrounded by
friends and a loving, supportive family. It's perhaps an unfair advantage for the person who happens to have the support of a loving
family, but whoever said life was fair?

Kids often have best friends: They seek out having a best friend.
Best friends work wonders for kids. It's not just that a best friend is
a child's favorite playmate, it's that knowing you have a best friend
gives you something to look forward to. A best friend breeds optimism and hopefulness—philosophies that are as essential in business as in every other aspect of life.

You don't negotiate against a computer. There are always people involved, some of whom are directly part of the negotiations,
some of whom are not. And some of the people on your own team
have complex, not always transparent objectives, just like you.
Would it be too bold to suggest that not everyone in every office in
America is a team player? Isn't it true that some of your coworkers
covet your office? To help protect you against these backstabbers,
you need friends. Friends are the only antidote to those who are

not your friends and who don't have your best interests at heart. True friendship, inside and outside of the office, can provide a number of substantial benefits:

- Friends can give you frank advice.

- Through friends, you have strength in numbers—you know that you're not the only one who believes what you believe.

- Friends provide emotional support, which even the strongest businessperson needs.

- Friends can inspire and help you to fight for what you want; in negotiations, they encourage you not to give up or compromise on what they know is most important to you.

Friends offer something else, too, that's a little less tangible but equally important: Because friendships also involve a lot of negotiations and suffer from highs and lows, friendships provide continual, if not subconscious, negotiating practice (as do marriages and families). As with many human activities, the more you do something, the better you get at it.

Give Yourself a Time-Out

If you're feeling down because things haven't been going well, your family life is in the pits and your kids hate you, then the best thing for you (and your company) may be to let somebody else do the heavy lifting until things get better for you.

Most people know that pilots have to undergo regular medical checkups. But what many people don't know is that pilots are supposed to take themselves off of active flight duty if they're feeling sick or mentally under the weather. Pilots perform a checklist, I'M SAFE, which stands for illness, medication, stress, alcohol, fatigue, and emotions. Pilots who can't give an okay to each of those items, personally validating that they are not impaired by any of those conditions, don't fly. Having a good support network of family and friends doesn't help with things like illness and alcohol (for pilots, that means having had a drink in the past eight hours), but knowing that you have good friends and family you can count on goes a long way toward reducing stress, the need for medication, and emotional issues.

Kids call off play dates (or their parents do it for them) when they don't have the energy level needed to deal with other people. An observant mom knows when her child is too fussy or stressed to enjoy a play date and would rather make the call to cancel than put her child on overload. But with adults, well, that's another story: Businessmen and businesswomen like to think of themselves as superheroes, able to endure the pains of coach seating for hours on end, willing to live out of a suitcase for days and days, and willing to crawl behind all sorts of furniture to connect to the Internet. You can visualize this scenario in your mind's eye: Two children are vying over a toy fire truck. One child's got a little fever and feels achy; the other is healthy and feisty. The answer to the question of which child's going to end up with the fire truck is indisputable.

If you're feeling sick or stressed you're going to make mistakes. Even if you're not thinking about other things—the problems in your love life, when you can get to use the bathroom next, whether you're going to watch the hotel movie this evening or just go directly to sleep—you're simply going to be subpar. Trying to be stoic is more often counterproductive than helpful. In your own childhood days you might have heard the ancient fable of the Spartan boy and the fox. The boy came upon a fox, captured the animal, and stuck it under his tunic. He knew that he wasn't permitted to have an animal and might be punished for it, so when the fox, hidden under his clothing, began to gnaw at his flesh, he remained stoic and did not utter a single cry. He was a model Spartan, suppressing the pain he felt—right up until the moment that the fox bit into a vital organ and killed him. Not exactly a model for modern people to emulate, however.

If you're feeling less than 100 percent—all right, maybe less than 90 percent, since it's rare for any of us to be 100 percent all the time—slow down the negotiations. You don't have to vacate the meeting, cancel the meeting, call in a substitute negotiator, or anything like that. Just slow it down. Discuss something that's not critical to the negotiation; get to know each other; talk about your company's history—just don't do anything critical while you're not at your best.

Parents are often able to use the excuse, "Johnny wasn't feeling very well—he was up coughing most of last night. That's why he didn't do well on his spelling test." But adults can't say to their boss: "Sorry, I blew the $5 million negotiation. I was still getting over that bout with Montezuma." Offering an excuse after the fact, well, that just seems lame.

What adults need to do is monitor their health and well-being on an ongoing basis. If you feel you're getting overwhelmed, take the break you need (the vacation, the sick days, the sabbatical) before you're called upon to undertake some difficult task. Then you'll come back to it, rested and ready.

The trouble is, vacation days must often be scheduled months in advance; sick days are limited; and sabbaticals don't even exist in many occupations. If you're in a position where you're not able to schedule time off when you need it most, then you'll have to look for ways to take care of yourself on weekends and before or after work. Some people take mini-vacations over the weekends, reserving time for themselves at a spa or at a romantic inn on a regular basis—perhaps once a month or every other month. That can be a real rejuvenator. Others claim the answer is to get a good night's sleep every night, regardless of what's going on at work. For these people, a special mattress or a particular type of foam pillow or a soundproof bedroom is what it takes to create a haven of peace every night. One idea that's been around for a while is the "power nap." Stressed-out businesspeople can learn to fall asleep in short intervals during the day, awakening refreshed and reenergized. Any of these techniques might work for you.

Let the Other Guy Think He's Won

It's a brilliant strategy. Read on.

Being a child has a number of things going for it. For one, you can fit in small spaces, which helps when the remote control has dropped behind the headboard and is lost under the bed. Okay, that's not too helpful when it comes to negotiations. But another thing about being a child is that your ego's not yet fully developed. You're not so concerned with saving face, maintaining a certain image. Self-image can be a killer: It gets in the way of so many things. Children have the luxury of negotiating without trying to live up to an image, and they are better off for it.

How does not having an ego help kids when they negotiate? The most significant way it contributes an advantage is that it allows children to use the strategy of letting the other guy think he's won—or, more accurately, not worrying about whether it *appears* that *you've* lost. Actually winning what you're after does matter, and if being mistaken for the loser works to your advantage, that's okay as far as children are concerned. If children are trading toys, they're interested in what they're interested in: That's why you often see one kid trading baseball cards for another kid's model car. Neither the appearance nor the reality of "winning" matters. In fact, helping the other side feel that they've won, by giving up things that you don't really want (for instance, if you no longer collect model cars), helps you achieve your goals.

Kids apply this technique very subtly. Here's a report from one parent, whose child won an argument by very cleverly tricking her mother into thinking she won:

My little master negotiator is my two-year-old daughter Noelle. I was intending to take her shopping for new shoes on Saturday. When I got her settled in the car seat, she asked where we were going, and the following conversation ensued:

"Shopping," was my reply.

"I say not," said the tyrant of the backseat.

"But we need to go to the store to get a few things."

"I say not. I want to swing."

"No, we are going shopping."

"I say not." At this point, she appealed to my mother, who was with us. "Mim, I not go shopping. I go to Pawpaw's house."

My mother, always the pushover, replied, "Okay, sweetie, but let's go to the store first. We need to get you new shoes."

"Not! I not want shoes. I want Pawpaw," the tyrant said again.

"Wouldn't you like to have some pretty new shoes? You need new shoes." This time it was my mother and I, two adults, pleading in unison. At this point, there was a moment of silence in the backseat. The toddler examined my face in the rearview mirror and then looked down at her feet. Suddenly, her face lit up.

"I got shoes on. Let's go Pawpaw's."
The battle was over. She won.

There was a certain synergy going on here. The little girl decided that the only way she could achieve her objective, going to her grandparents' house instead of shoe shopping, would be to try and get her mother to believe that the ultimate objective would be achieved by *merely putting on* shoes. Her mother certainly recognized the difference between buying new shoes and putting on shoes, but the little girl figured—and was right on the money about this—that her mother would accept this change. The strategy of changing the rules would not have worked unless the little girl knew (or guessed) that her mother would cave in to the change of objective.

Can you make this method work in the business world? Oh, yes. Of course, it won't be as easy as it was for this toddler. She had the advantage of having an adversary who really wasn't prepared to fight about the shoes. Across a real bargaining table, you're going to have to come up with some kind of plausible alternative that will allow your counterparts to imagine that they're walking away with a victory. This happens all the time in politics: When defeat on a particular bill draws near, all a legislator has to do is redefine the objective to be able to declare victory.

Modifying the rules so that the other side thinks it's won—or gotten something important—is one way to apply this technique. Simply making sure that the other side doesn't lose or is happy with what it gets, all the same, is another way. In an August 8, 2004 article ("The Poker Player") in *The New York Times,* Brian Roberts, CEO of Comcast Corp., said: "I've been able to perpetuate what my dad started. He always told me that in any negotiation, let the other guy feel [as if] he won. Don't take the last nickel from the table." Letting the other side win—a little or a lot, depending on what you can offer—can help you secure what you want.

There's something else I want to mention about this technique. Getting her mother to think that she won the argument was part of the little girl's strategy, but the girl also added a dash of "changing the rules," another technique discussed in a separate chapter. Often, these techniques are not independent, but part of a continuum of strategies. Sometimes you need to add the smidgen of another strategy to make your technique work effectively. How did this girl change the rules? By slightly redefining the goal from buying new shoes to putting on shoes.

Break the Rules

Before we get any further into the merits of changing the rules, let me cover the more extreme application first: breaking the rules. After all, as that old cliché goes, rules were made to be broken. Children love that line—especially when they're up against a rule they don't like. It's a rite of passage to test the rules and find out which ones aren't enforced. (Witness the administration of George W. Bush and its efforts to ignore, contravene, and rewrite the Geneva convention regarding the treatment of prisoners.)

Sometimes breaking the rules is inadvertent—who knows all the rules for everything? (Right on red, but only after a full stop and not into a two-way street—but that's only for certain states.) Rules may be so complex and even contradictory that it is impossible to follow them all the time. There's a running joke in aviation: If you follow all the Federal Aviation Administration regulations you'll never have an accident. True. But you'll never get off the ground, either. (That's the joke part.) The impossibility of obeying all the rules all of the time—be they society's laws or a business's rules—means that at some time or other, you will have to make a semiconscious or deliberate decision to violate a rule (maybe even several times during any given day). It's not a matter of whether you might do it: You *will* break rules. And this has nothing to do with how ethical you may be. Society and the business world are so complex that even the most ethical and decent human beings are going to break the rules now and then.

That's different, of course, from breaking the rules on purpose. But just as it's true that you must violate some laws, regulations, rules, and customs during your day-to-day life, it's also true that not all laws, regulations, rules, and customs are, in themselves, just or moral—or even a good idea. Within the guidelines of morality, your conscience, and what society allows, you can decide that breaking certain rules is justified and necessary in your business life.

The party you're negotiating with may or may not be completely versed in what the rules are, either—and that may be one of the discoveries you can use to your advantage. If the other side— your boss, perhaps—is very busy, she may not have the time to keep up on all the company's rules. But that doesn't mean that she won't look them up if she needs to. So be cautious to test your limits when using this technique.

That caveat aside, testing is worthwhile: Probing how timid or hesitant your negotiating opponent is will give you a sense of how far you can push and how tough you can be during an actual negotiation. In order to know whether you need to "sweat the small stuff," you need to learn whether you're dealing with a loosey-goosey crowd or are among people who are sticklers for propriety in every area. If you break a minor rule and your boss, contractual partner, or colleague points out your transgression, you know that the "break the rules" advice won't work for you in this situation. But if your environment is more like the Wild West than a tightly run ship, well, pardner, make the most of it.

Which brings me to an important point about testing the other side before you break any rules: Do it well in advance of negotiations. You need to find out what you can about the other side's attention to detail and probe their attitudes about rule-keeping before you start doing anything they might consider off-limits. When you were a child and you stayed at a friend's house, you learned that you had to observe the rules where you were. The same holds true now that you're an adult. If your mother wouldn't let you sleep in your clothes but it's fine with the mom at the sleepover party, then sure, sleep in your clothes. But if the parents hosting the sleepover expect you to make your bed in the morning—something your own parents never asked you to do—then you'd better be prepared to do it right, hospital corners and all.

How do find out what the rules are in each situation . . . and which ones can be safely broken? Again, you do what kids do: You gently, but regularly, test the other side's will, resolve, and views by crossing the artificial line created by "the rules." If this technique sounds vague and imprecise, with no clear objective delineated, that's because all of those things are true: Testing the other side is just that—you're poking it with a stick just a little bit to see what happens. You need to keep your ears and eyes open for whatever reactions ensue, because they may not be all that obvious to you. Not every negotiating tool should be reserved for the actual negotiations—people who anticipate that they will have to negotiate at some point in the future and who plan for those unknown but inevitable negotiations often win.

One last point: Expect to be tested yourself. Some people do this by design; others because they retain some childlike qualities. While you'll have an advantage over your opponents (or negotiating partners) by knowing how these techniques work, you may also find that many other people use these kid-negotiation techniques too, either innately or because they resemble another negotiating skill they are familiar with.

Change the Rules

Although some aspects of this negotiating technique were just covered, I'm including some additional information about it, in part because we adults like to have things compartmentalized in folders, computer directories, and even book chapters. While breaking the rules is a separate technique, you may need to tone it down, depending on your business environment, so that you're merely changing or revisiting the rules.

Children are notorious for ignoring "the rules." They talk loudly in restaurants. They treat a newly painted wall as a canvas for their finger-painting. They like to run up and down the aisles of grocery stores.

Children may know the rules of the adult world—because you've told them a million times—but that doesn't mean those are the rules they have to play by. Your admonishment, "Be quiet in church," often changes to, "If you can sit quietly during the service, I'll take you out for ice cream afterward." See what's happened? By chafing under the adult's rule, the child has won something she wouldn't have otherwise. Children *know* that *you* have to obey the rules, and they know it's worth something to them to get you to agree to a negotiated settlement that's more to their liking.

We're often told to "think outside the box" or "color outside the lines." Even better is making your own box. If you're creative enough to come up with new rules that result in a more useful sort of box or a more spectacularly colored picture, no one will resent you for taking liberties with the old rules. They'll celebrate you as a visionary, an innovator, someone to be emulated. Until, of course, the new rules you invented become stale, and someone else needs to come along and rewrite them to create a new and better design.

Follow the Rules to the Letter

There's a television commercial in which a boy who's maybe ten years old is bothering his sister by lying right next to her on the beach. Ugh—cooties! The girl appeals to her parents, who are relaxing in beach chairs nearby, to tell her brother not to touch her. The brother obliges, and for the rest of the commercial he hovers over his sister with his finger a fraction of an inch away from her, saying, "I'm not touching you, I'm not touching you, I'm not touching you." Anyone watching this commercial has immediate sympathy for the girl and certainly wouldn't mind if she smacked him.

So the brother is literally sticking to the terms of his agreement, but in so doing, he's driving his sister crazy. Being a child, that's probably his goal. Being an adult, you'll have a worthier goal in mind when you use this technique.

Here's how I used this technique in a contract dispute with a former employee. The former employee had her husband, a lawyer, call us to argue on her behalf. It so happened that her husband worked for the government, and he had called us from his office, leaving a message on my office voice mail that included his government title—an attempt to scare us into thinking that he could investigate us from his position as a government lawyer. Once I told him that I would make an issue of his improper use of his office (implying it was as if he had threatened to bring the weight of the United States government to bear on a private business matter), he had to worry that I was going to report his actions to his supervisor. Although I knew full well that he had not been speaking as a government employee, what mattered is that he had, in fact, violated the rules regarding the use of his government title. We could make the case to his superiors that he was guilty of abuse of the government's power. He had broken the rule, and even though we hadn't really been intimidated by his use of his title, we could demand that his superiors start an investigation of our complaint—because a rule's a rule. We were no longer arguing over the issue the ex-employee had raised; now the argument had shifted to something I knew I could win, because he'd been caught breaking a rule.

Be Naive

Appearing naive and following the rules to the letter are very different strategies that may achieve the same effect: They frustrate the other side. I call this the "Joey Syndrome," named for the lovable but somewhat dim character on the television series *Friends*. Joey often got what he wanted not through the logic of his arguments, the force of his personality, or any other traditional method. He got his way because people thought he was genuinely perplexed and needed their help in some way.

We've all encountered this pattern in our lives—especially when talking with children. They can't be expected to handle everything on their own. No matter how slowly you speak, how simple the words are that you choose, or how much you do to get them started, you have to do more. And more. And then you end up doing their whole job for them—they don't need to lift a finger.

I recently saw this happen on a flight from London to the United States. An elderly couple was seated behind us; they didn't speak English, and you could tell from they way they gripped the back of the seats in front of them—our seats—throughout the entire flight that this was their first time on an airplane. In what was perhaps the most clichéd moment I have ever experienced, the flight attendant asked these passengers if they wanted some coffee. They didn't understand and smiled blankly. So she asked in a louder voice, "Would you like some coffee?" They still didn't reply, so the flight attendant spoke even more loudly: "DO YOU WANT COFFEE?" Finally, she realized it was no good trying to take an order. She came back with both coffee and tea and let them point to what they wanted. Then she served them immediately; they didn't have to wait for their order to be filled. Now I'm pretty sure that this elderly couple wasn't using this technique to get served ahead of everyone else, but the effect was the same: The flight attendant just gave up because she got frustrated with the apparent inability of the other party to understand her.

Nobody has unlimited patience or time. Eventually the other party will either give in and do what's needed to complete the deal, or walk away. The couple on the airplane could easily have ended up with nothing. But because they were smiling and not demanding—just sweet but somewhat befuddled travelers—the flight attendant served them first.

But here's the risk in this strategy: If it becomes apparent that you *do* understand, but just aren't cooperating, the other side will walk away—and probably tell others that you're a faker. If you present yourself as charmingly, helplessly naive, it helps to really be that way.

Yet sometimes in business, that's just what you want. When you've got a persistent salesman who keeps calling, it's in your interest to be unable to comprehend what he's trying to sell. "So let me see," the potential customer says. "If we take the car with five years' additional service warranty"—which, by the way, is what you've already decided you don't want or need—"we get a brand-new computer and you need to fix our old one for free if something goes wrong?" It's one thing to negotiate over the price of a purchase, but sometimes the deal gets so dragged out with attempted sales of extras that this negotiating technique is called for. When you're the naive one, the negotiations aren't about facts, or money, or position, or power, or anything substantive: They're over—well, that's the problem—*they're never over.* The only way you are going to end the discussion is when you make clear that no amount of explanation is going to get the salesman anywhere.

Perhaps this negotiating tool is most useful in avoiding negotiations that you don't want to enter into altogether. Think about it: How do you negotiate with somebody who doesn't understand what the purpose of the negotiating process is? How do you negotiate with somebody who doesn't seem to have the ability to grasp the intricate details of what's involved in making a deal? In other words, how do you negotiate with a child? You can't. So you cut your losses and stop bothering the person. You think you're wasting your time—and you are. And the naive one has stopped you from wasting *his* time, too. The naive party has caught you in a brilliant trap.

Go Out of Your Way to Please the Other Side

Some kids—though certainly not all—do whatever they can to please their friends. These are nice kids, happy kids, kids that others want to be around. There's a good deal of psychobabble about how children (and adults) who seek to make others happy have low self-esteem. There's even a group therapy exercise in which you have to put a dollar in the "loony bin" every time you say "thank you" when you don't mean it—that is, every time you say "thanks" reflexively. Pleasing others is considered a disability and a liability when it comes to dealing with other people.

I disagree. Making the other side happy, comfortable, and content is not a sign of weakness; it's not a psychological disorder that indicates you have some deep-seated problem. Rather, it can be a simple, even elegant, way to ease tensions and put others in a mood to be receptive to your ideas. You do not become subservient or a "doormat" simply because you bestow little courtesies on others; you come across as gracious and pleasant, setting a cordial tone at the outset, making it apparent that you anticipate the development of a warm and mutually respectful relationship.

This is what children learn to do when the put on their "Sunday best" and their "Sunday manners" (or the appropriate cultural equivalent for those without observances on Sundays). Now this isn't natural behavior for children by any means, but it certainly is useful, and it's a shame that so many children, as they grow older, start to look down on the idea of formality and good manners.

One of the reasons this technique can be so successful is that the other side may not expect to be treated with super-politeness. They'll probably be caught off guard. They may jump to the conclusion that you are servile and fawning and thus easy to manipulate. So when you come back at them in negotiations with your hard-nosed terms—gently draped as they are in the rhetoric of courtesies—they may not even notice how the substance is in your favor.

Let's also consider one of the more commonplace uses of extravagant politeness: Just think about the last time you were stopped for speeding. (You haven't *ever* been stopped for speeding? Then remember when you were searched at airport security.) If you handled yourself right, you addressed the officer as "sir" or "ma'am" at every utterance. You didn't curse, whine, or try to play the officer for a fool. You were the model of cooperation. Your every gesture made clear that you did not want to do anything to hinder the officer from doing his duty. You just wanted to do your best to help. If you succeeded in being humble enough and gracious enough—and the officer you were dealing with was sufficiently pleased to be shown some rare respect, instead of being treated, as usual, as just an oaf with a badge—you found you were allowed to continue on your way, either with just a warning (for the speeding stop) or without having to give up your favorite pair of nail scissors (that you forgot to pack in your checked luggage).

Be Needy

Kids are often able to position themselves well to win negotiations because they *need* adults. You have to help them buy clothes, feed them, make their beds. That's the nature of childhood (especially when it comes to younger kids). They just can't do that much for themselves. You, the parent, *must* do certain things for them.

Try as you might, asking a two-year-old to make her own macaroni and cheese is going to make your kitchen resemble modern art. Sticky modern art, at that. The child wins because there is no other way that the negotiation can be successfully concluded. Although the timing is something that can (sometimes) be negotiated, who actually does the work is preordained. You might delay feeding your daughter by twenty minutes, but ultimately you are the one who's going to make the meal. (Trying to negotiate the time in the face of other child-negotiating techniques, such as throwing a tantrum, may also be difficult! Kids often combine negotiating techniques or use their various techniques in quick succession.)

You might think that adults can't appear needy; that showing yourself to be unable to do something without the help of somebody else puts you in an inferior position. While this can certainly be the case, it's not always going to be true that you lose if you appear weak. Even some of the most hardened executives harbor a desire at least to explain and show others the ropes, if not to outright help them. People feel better about themselves (this is the enlightened view of humankind) when they can help others; people feel superior and more potent (the cynical perspective) when they can show that they're more capable or knowledgeable than others. When you have legitimate needs that must be met before a deal can go forward, then it's in the other side's interest to help you—just as it is in that parent's interest to make lunch for her hungry child. If you don't have the skills, experience, background, adequate staff, or intellect (from your negotiating partner's perspective), the other side has a dilemma: They must either provide you with the support you need or abandon you. That's a huge risk, of course, and so you should choose this strategy only after having calculated the equation from the other side's point of view. Make sure you know that you have enough to offer so that abandonment is not an option. As with most of these childhood-based negotiating techniques, there's a need for a levelheaded, very adult sort of analysis before proceeding.

Once you are set on this course, and if you are successful at this strategy, here are some of the things you can expect the other side to do for you:

- Lend you staff

- Give you access to their technical skills

- Show you how to do things your company couldn't have done before

Instead of making the negotiations just that, a negotiation, you have added another element: The negotiations are now a teaching exercise and/or support effort. With needy kids, parents either do whatever it is they need for them or painstakingly try to teach them how to do it. (Remember giving shoelace-tying lessons to your kids? How many times did you simply end up tying their shoes for them, just to speed things up?)

Remember, being needy isn't the same as being weak; it's a way to gain more expertise or have a burden you can't handle shared by somebody else, which helps your company to conserve resources and build skills, so that in the end you emerge much stronger.

Something to consider before you set out on this course: Being needy changes the nature of the relationship you have with your negotiating partner. It prevents you from assuming the status of an equal. You put yourself in the position of the junior partner, the one in need of mentoring, and it will become difficult, if not impossible, to be viewed as other than the junior partner—at least in that particular relationship—on into the future. However, as you or your company grows and benefits from the help you've received over time from that relationship, you will be able to enter into other business arrangements as either an equal or even the superior partner yourself.

Ask the Person Who's Most Likely to Say "Yes"

All children quickly learn that there is no unified, single mind known as "The Parent." There is Mommy and there is Daddy, and they have different personalities, interests, and abilities. Sometimes it's better to ask Mommy something; sometimes it's better to ask Daddy. In our house, I'm the person who's lenient about getting to bed at night, but I'm a terror when it comes to leaving for school on time in the morning. My wife, Peggy, is the opposite. So which parent do you think our children will turn to when they want to play for "just another five minutes" and it's past nine o'clock?

Here's what one parent told me: "My toddler responds to discipline from my husband far better than he does from me. If my husband gets after him for something, sometimes he will run over to me for 'comfort' or 'sympathy.'"

When you negotiate with somebody, it's important to make sure that you're negotiating with the right somebody. Clearly you want to ensure that the person you're negotiating with has the authority—or access to the right authority—to make decisions. (The child knows that it's no good to ask Grandma if you can have a dog, since Grandma only serves an advisory function.)

Not only does that person have to have the authority to give you what you want, but two other conditions may have to be met as well:

- They have to be willing to use that authority.

- They have to be willing to back it up under possible pressure to reverse the decision from some other person that you could have asked but didn't.

Children quickly discover this trick, and so they grow to expect that the strategy may fail on either count, as in this example: 1) After Mom said "no" to sewing a new Halloween costume but Dad said "yes," it turned out that Dad didn't know how to help make the costume—so no new costume; or 2) Dad said "yes," meaning he would try to get Mom to reverse her decision about not sewing a new Halloween costume this year, but Mom was able to withstand his pressure, and so her "no" held firm.

Adults discover that these limitations apply to business situations, too. You might be able to get the head of one division of a company to agree to help develop a new product, but then the head of the actual production unit says, "No go." Or you get the head of the production unit to agree to make a prototype, but then the chief financial officer overrules the decision on the grounds of a budget crunch.

Children are usually stuck when either one parent or the other says no. But adults in business usually have more options. You might be able to lobby the person saying no by marshaling the facts and figures to make the case that one party has already approved. You might be able to enlist other allies that can make your case for you (a variant of the "get your gang to stand by you" strategy discussed earlier in this book). A project or a negotiation will almost always involve multiple decision makers with varying degrees of influence over the outcome.

One way to help ensure the success of the strategy is to scope out the situation well before you make your first pitch so that you can choose the person most likely to react positively from the start. Then let that person approach the next person that he or she thinks can be persuaded to support the project. Ask each new ally to bring in others. By the time you get to those you are most worried will turn you down, you'll have built up momentum for acceptance. You'll have created a feeling that consensus already exists.

Children do this when seeking permission for things that other parents have allowed but their own parents have forbidden. The child says, "All my friends' parents let them go to the mall on their own." Parents tend to respond with the classic and indisputable argument: "If all your friends' parents let them jump off the Brooklyn Bridge, do you think that would make us let you do so, too?" At this point, if the child is savvy, she doesn't argue further. She can see her new task is to make her parents aware that going to the mall without a supervising adult present is not at all the same as jumping off the Brooklyn Bridge. And the person to make that case is one of those responsible parents of a friend who has allowed her child to go with friends to the mall and can attest that her trust has not turned out to be misplaced. However, if the child is bluffing and the reality is that very few parents of children she knows are actually allowing their kids to go to the mall unaccompanied—or if the parents who have allowed their children to go shopping on their own have ended up with outrageous bills from stores, or the kids have been caught smoking at the mall—then the child is probably going to lose the negotiations on the merits.

The fact is, children are seldom as skilled at using this tactic as an adult would be, because children lack the foresight and the judg-ment to analyze the data and figure out in advance if they can build a winning case. They claim all other parents are permitting something, when all a mom or a dad needs to do is make a few phone calls to discover that's not true. But as an adult, you can avoid these kinds of pitfalls—now that you've been warned.

Play One Side Against the Other

This is a variant of "Ask the parent most likely to say yes," but with a slightly more devilish twist. You're not looking for one authority to persuade another to do things your way; you think they might cancel each other out. Playing two sides off each other can be an effective negotiating tool, especially if there are three or more parties to the talks. A skillful negotiator—a child—knows how to do this well. Adults, well, not so well (at least not yet).

My seven-year-old daughter, Claire, wanted to bring home two newly hatched chicks from her classroom for the weekend. This was fine with me, but I knew it was not high on a list of things my wife wanted to do. From her previous kindergarten experience with a guinea pig, Claire knew that her mother was unenthusiastic, because Mom was the one who ended up cleaning out the cage. So Claire came to me first to ask if she could take the chicks home: "Please. Please. Please," she wheedled. "I'll help clean the cage, I really will." I knew she couldn't do it herself and that one parent would probably end up doing all the real dirty work. And I also figured, again, that my wife would be the one to handle it . . . but once the chicks were here, and she saw how cute they were and how much Claire enjoyed having them, she really wouldn't mind. "Well, okay, as long as it's okay with Mommy," I responded. Little did I realize what Claire would do with my conditional assent. She went straight to her mother and told her that I'd said okay to the chicks and I would take care of all the cage cleaning! As soon as my wife heard that I'd taken on the chore entirely, she agreed to the deal. By the time we each realized how we'd been played off each other, the chicks were here—and we both ended up cleaning the cage—with our daughter's help, of course (limited though it was). But in the end we weren't sorry: She did love having those chicks at home!

Children use this strategy all the time. They know that their parents disagree: Because their parents aren't in complete harmony about a particular issue, their chances of getting what they want are many times better if both parents argue about it, otherwise the opposed parent may have first shot at the decision. In the normal course of events, the advantage goes to the side that wants the status quo; the onus is on the side that needs to muster enough support to effect a change. But by exploiting the differences between the parties, the child may be able to tip the balance in favor of the child's desired end.

If there's no natural inclination for one parent to agree, the child must coax one parent to the child's side. What's important to note about this strategy is that the child doesn't have to dilute his energy by trying to get both parents to say yes—one parent, once that parent has been induced to argue in the child's stead, will do.

In business, you need to find your campaigner, too. Often there's an individual who will benefit from the deal going through—or has a lot to lose if the deal doesn't go through. If you start buying a lot of calendars from a company, for example, the person who runs that company's calendar department may get a bigger budget: That is the person you want to approach. Often somebody in the company you're negotiating with can be a stronger booster than you can.

Delay Matters (Or "I Have to Ask My Mommy")

When kids say, "I have to ask my mommy," they mean it. When car salesmen say, "I have to talk to my manager," we know that they don't mean it (which is a nice way to say that we *know* that they are lying), but we let them get away with it.

Why? Why do smart, savvy adults let sleazy car salesmen get away with this childlike negotiating tactic, even when we know better? There's no good answer other than we do. (Okay, not all of us fall for this one, but then nothing in the realm of human interaction is a constant.) A partial answer is that we're caught by surprise by this tactic (how you can be surprised after your third car purchase is another question), and that we're not quick-witted enough to say to the car salesman, "No. If you're not able to negotiate with me yourself, I'm leaving." So the tactic winds its way down to its inevitable conclusion—it wears you down.

Delay, delay, delay. Asking one's mommy isn't about seeking permission from a higher authority—it's really about delay. Slowing down the negotiations works to your advantage because it tires out and frustrates the other side. They're left alone with their thoughts, and thinking inevitably leads to worry. People worry because there's an unseen decision maker involved in the process—an unpredictable element. And worry leads people to want to come to some arrangement, even if it's not the best deal you could possibly get.

Move Slowly and Procrastinate

You can use the "I have to ask mommy" technique, as discussed previously, to bring about a needed delay, or you can delay by any number of other means. Kids are masters of the art of procrastination. They may not understand the strategic applications of what they're doing, however. They're just plain old kids, after all, who like to put off the unpleasant or prolong something enjoyable, like a play date, when the parents are ready to go home. A lot of the time it just seems that they plain won't do what you want them to do. We call it dawdling; they call it victory.

Let's say you're off to the shoe store and your daughter doesn't want to get new shoes: It's a scary place, the shoe store is. So she's slow to dress. She's slow to brush her teeth. (When have you ever not had to remind her to brush her teeth?) She insists on having her hair put into a fancy braid. You make it to the car, but then the car seat is uncomfortable. And the inevitable: "I forgot my blankie!" And that's if you're driving to the shoe store. If you have a store that you can walk to, you're going to find that your daughter's feet move as if they weigh hundreds of pounds each.

Kids succeed at procrastination for several reasons. First, they haven't yet internalized adult concepts, such as "Time is money" or "We haven't got all day." They really do think they've got all the time in the world. Second, they don't worry too much about coming across as inefficient planners when they call for a delay for something they should have done earlier. When your four-year-old says, "Wait, I have to go to the potty," you may fire back, "You should have done that a half hour ago when I first suggested it"— but you can't really get too mad about it; you know your child is still learning about timing of bathroom breaks.

Adults, on the other hand, are far more limited in their use of procrastination. Adults, for obvious reasons, aren't going to want to come across as oblivious to the time constraints of others. No adult in his right mind would offer up as an excuse for delay, "Gee, it took me a long time to tie my shoes this morning." Even the tried-and-true adult-type delaying tactics—"I was caught in traffic," "There's an emergency call from my family," and various types of home or car repair misadventures—can be countered, sometimes quite easily. The other side points out, "We could have set up a conference call so that you could participate." Or, "We would have sent a car service to pick you up." Or, "We would have faxed the papers over to you or e-mailed them to you—we could have wrapped up this business any number of other ways."

To show how delaying can work to your disadvantage, especially if not done with finesse, consider the Michael Jackson case. Twice he failed to show up on time in court. The first time the judge let it go. The second time—despite the offered excuse that Jackson had been in the hospital—the judge issued an arrest warrant and only in the last five minutes decided not to revoke the latecomer's bail for the remainder of the trial.

So the message is clear: Adults, use this technique sparingly, and be sure your delaying tactics are plausible. Anticipate the likely objections that may be offered by the party who's been made to wait. Only embark on this course if you are sure of the benefits that you will reap from gaining that extra time. Here's a valid, though perhaps extreme, case in point. You are the attorney in the case of client on death row. You've lost all the previous rounds of appeal to the courts. Your client's only hope now is for the governor to grant clemency. But you know there are still facts about the case that could save your client if uncovered in time. If your delaying tactics fail, your client dies. If you succeed, then there's a chance that he'll not only stay alive but be exonerated of the crime altogether. How could you not look for every possible reason to slow the process down?

Do a Bad Job

I have a friend who has successfully integrated this technique into his entire life. Once, years and years ago when he was first married, Roger was asked by his wife to do the dishes. (This is a true story, by the way.) He did a bad job. Now anybody can do a bad job with the dishes, but doing a passable job isn't hard, either. Roger never could get those dishes clean—even with a dishwasher. So, after some weeks of marriage, Roger's wife stopped asking him to do the dishes. Roger had succeeded.

Kids use the same technique when it comes to cleaning their rooms. Some of them are good cleaners; other kids learn that the worse they do, the more likely it is that somebody (a parent) will finish the job for them. Children also use this technique when it comes to homework, but unlike knowing how to clean a room, knowing algebra is actually important. (Really, it is!)

If you do a bad job in something, nobody is going to ask you to continue doing it anymore. It requires a sacrifice of ego to deliberately do something badly because your colleagues and coworkers *are* going to think less of you. Your status and prowess will be diminished—at least as far as that particular task is concerned.

There is only one sure way to use this technique: You must do something else *exceptionally* well. Kids are able to get away with not ever cleaning their rooms because they are exceptional at being much-loved sons and daughters. But chances are that you're not going to have a boss who will love you for your adorable self alone, as a parent loves a sometimes naughty child. So, if you decide to do badly at some task as a way to show your boss that it should never have been assigned to you in the first place, you'd better be pretty darn good at whatever it is that you need to do, whether it is technical support or analysis or finding the lowest-cost supplier or winning customers.

The question is: What is this technique good for? The answer is that doing a bad job is a minor negotiating technique that can help to position you properly within your own organization. It's used for lateral movement, not significant negotiations. It's certainly not for someone who aims to end up at the top; it's far better suited to someone who loves what he does and doesn't want to be transferred away and made to do something else.

Make a Deal That You Can Exchange for a Better Deal Later

Kids use this practice fairly frequently, but adults hardly ever do. Adults tend to become focused on the long-term objective and worry that if they accept something less than their objective, they'll lose out on the chance to get it later. So they hold out too long and miss the chance for any deal, rather than settle for less than a perfect deal. (Could this be the real reason the Middle East peace negotiations keep falling apart?)

Kids, on the other hand, frequently "sign" deals and use them as leverage later on. Let me give you an example. Your child wants you to read her *Watership Down,* a long and, depending on your perspective, overrated novel. She discovered the novel and became interested because the story is about bunnies. You agree to read it to her when she's "old enough," thinking that she'll either forget or, more likely, lose interest in the course of the year that you've asked her to wait. You're wrong. Believe me, you're wrong. A year comes and goes, Ellen reminds you, and then what? You either have to read the entire novel out loud or you have to agree to something else. That something else might be reading *Harry Potter,* or it might be buying her the book on tape. You quickly agree to whatever reasonable terms she suggests because you know she settled for less than what she could have obtained if she'd kept fighting. Her seeming acquiescence the year before left her in a strengthened position that gets her what she wants when "the deal" comes up for renegotiation.

Why did you agree to read the book to her aloud in the first place? Well, for one thing, you knew that Ellen was too young to understand it, so you weren't going to have to read it at the time, which your brain interpreted as "ever." Second, you wanted to please her, to make her smile; agreeing to something that wasn't meaningful or problematic to you at the time was an easy way to keep her happy.

In the adult world, you're most likely to use this technique in contract negotiations. Lawyers add clauses to contracts to cover various contingencies and to correct the mistakes of previous contracts. *Clever* lawyers put in clauses that can be used later on—years from now, perhaps—as negotiating tools. Clever lawyers know that circumstances change over time and that parts of contacts that seem irrelevant today may take on significance later. As you're negotiating, throw in those clauses. You'll be surprised how many farfetched conditions and terms you can include; any of them have the potential to turn into negotiating tools later on.

Here's where imagination, as well as basic business instincts, can be a powerful tool. Those people who foresaw the growth of the home computer and cellular telephone industries became very rich. They looked forward and had imagination. As you negotiate today's deal, think about what might be down the road for you. Be careful not to limit your options, and not to let the other side limit them, either.

Win Through Sympathy

When your child's been injured, suffered a disappointment, or had a bad day at school or on the playground, you do your best to make up for the loss, even if it means saying yes to something that would ordinarily rate a "no." That extra cookie, the ten minutes more of playtime—anything to put a smile back on that sad, sad face. It doesn't take children long to discover how advantageous it can be to have things go wrong.

The same thing is often true in business, though you won't be able to capitalize on your misfortunes quite as easily as a child can. You can't walk into a business meeting complaining that Mr. Howell was mean to you or that you never got your turn at the Xerox machine. Your tale of woe needs to be something that will elicit genuine nods of understanding. It must rise above the merely whiny into the truly miserable. Only then will you earn your "sympathy points."

Two caveats: Your sufferings can't be made up. As children quickly discover, wild tales are too easily unraveled, and then you lose credibility. And you can't pull this trick too often. If you're always claiming to be the victim of injustice, your business associates will soon realize that you're really a deserving victim.

Act Forlorn

This technique is akin to angling for sympathy, discussed previously, but without dragging in your personal life. This is a pure business strategy. You make the point that unless you get the concessions you need, you're in danger of losing everything, with consequences that hurt your negotiating partner, too.

Children use this technique when they ask to be passed onto a higher grade despite having failed a course. The teacher or the school system may grant the request because it hurts the school's overall performance evaluation whenever a child is held back. Big corporations play the forlorn card with even greater success: When Chrysler was about to go under in 1979, its executives appealed successfully to Congress for bailout loans to save the jobs of thousands of workers and prevent a big downturn in the automobile industry as a whole.

You might think that if you put yourself in the forlorn position, presenting yourself as the poor little orphan in need of rescue in a storm, you'll never be able to hold your head up again. But just look at what can happen. Years later, many of the corporations that had to beg for bailout money are reaping huge profits. And some of those kids who were promoted to the next grade have gone on to graduate with honors. (A far rarer occurrence, I grant you, but the cases do exist.) It's essential that after you've had the rescue that you negotiated, you fulfill your end of the bargain by doing your part to avoid the same pitfalls that put you there in the first place.

Change the Subject

Changing the subject is the thing to do when the subject at hand is something that puts you at a disadvantage. Changing the subject can also be used in tandem with delaying tactics as a way to derail negotiations when they're charging full steam ahead to a conclusion you don't want to reach. Changing the subject can throw you off on a tangent that needs to be explored, giving your side the time it needs to come up with alternatives that might be accepted.

Children change subjects almost at random; non sequiturs come naturally to them. Sometimes children lose sight of the main subject and start discussing another randomly introduced subject, possibly forgetting all about the first subject altogether. Children being teased sometimes discover the worth of this tactic. The subject at hand may be Henry's unzipped fly. Immediately after zipping up, Henry notices a foul smell in the air and accuses someone else of "cutting the cheese." Then all the children are busy pointing fingers at each other and holding their noses.

You wouldn't think a tactic so juvenile would work among adults, but it does. When it involves people changing the subject from an accusation hurled at them to a new and different accusation that they throw at someone else, the strategy is generally covered under the saying, "The best defense is a good offense." You could make the case that this is the tack that President Clinton's opponents took when they went after flaws in his personal life rather than policies implemented by his administration—the adult equivalent of "Billy's pee-pee is showing!"

Changing the subject isn't something that you can use in all circumstances (remember, none of these techniques work for every kind of negotiation). It works best when you know that you're negotiating in a hostile environment. When you're in a situation where you're outnumbered, where the other side wants to berate you or complain about you or get you to completely change your point of view, the best thing you can do is to change the subject and make them answer some other question entirely. Raise a small legal point that might require some research that will take a few days to complete. When changing the subject is masterfully done, you can take the other side completely by surprise and prevent the opposition from even playing their opening move. At worst, you gain yourself a little breathing room before the others come back to the original subject that you'd rather avoid.

Give Your Business "Lemonade Stand" Appeal

Children *always* do well with their lemonade stands. Have you ever heard of a child whose lemonade stand lost money? Even when there are four competing lemonade stands within a six-block radius, they all make money. Selling lemonade might be the only business in America that is guaranteed to make money.* Why is that? Because the customers are so eager to be supportive of those enterprising kids that they'll buy lemonade even when they aren't thirsty. They'll buy from each lemonade stand along the way to the beach. They never complain about the price or the lemonade formula that's overly sweet or too sour. These customers are endlessly forgiving simply because they know they're dealing with children. People *want* children to succeed.

You can't become a child again to recapture the customer's endless goodwill, but you can look for other ways to store up goodwill from the people you do business with.

---

* The exception may be Las Cruces, New Mexico, where city officials required four young girls to jump through multiple regulatory hoops to set up a lemonade stand.

One way is to make sure your business is linked to good deeds in your community. Your business should donate generously to school fund-raising auctions, support the scout troops, adopt a highway or park, plant trees, or donate a bench at the senior center. You should get your business's name listed every time supporters are being sought for community benefits and events. People may not remember every single good deed you do, but they'll have a sense of which businesses are community-oriented and which just come in, try to grab the biggest profit in the shortest time, and then leave.

Let me give you an example of how a business used its community appeal to its advantage. Down the street from my house is a block of shops that included an ice cream parlor. The owner was well known and beloved in the neighborhood as a guy who loved his work, loved the neighborhood he served, and supported all the local schools and causes. He knew all his customers and their families. One day the landlord announced a plan to redevelop the whole block. He wanted to kick out all the small businesses first, but most of them had leases with renewal options. He raised the rent each year until finally he drove most of the businesses out. The owner of the ice cream store, however, was stubborn. He didn't want to move and he didn't want to keep paying the increased rent. So he posted a sign in the window letting all his customers know his plight. The customers—especially the children—rallied around the ice cream store. They came to zoning committee meetings and neighborhood community association meetings and spoke out about the desire the keep their neighborhood ice cream vendor. Many of the customers signed a petition aimed at preventing the block from being developed. Although, ultimately, the ice cream seller did have to move, he won at least a two-year reprieve because the community showed support for his position, and when he eventually did relocate, he was able to persuade a high percentage of his customers to travel to his new location to patronize his shop.

Solicit a Bribe

Early on, children learn that if they stand their ground, they'll often be offered something if they instead do what their parent wants. This something is what parents call "a bribe" and what businesses call an "incentive." Raise your hand, parents, if you've ever given your child a reward during potty training. Okay, you can *all* put your hands down, now. Children catch on quickly: All they have to do is hold out for what they want and they might be offered a little something extra for doing what they knew they'd have to do in the end. And if their parents don't offer a bribe, the child can always say, "Last time I went pee-pee in the potty you give me a sticker." (Without parents, how else would the sticker business thrive?)

The same system works in business: Why settle for a little something when you can have more? If you're buying widgets for cash, wouldn't it be nice to have a "sample" of that company's new super-widget, too? Soliciting bribes works especially well when you're close to closing a deal: Keep those pants up and refuse to go near that potty until you see that sticker.

The key thing here is to make sure that everyone knows what you're doing. When I use the term "bribe," I mean that only figuratively: What you're doing is asking for something that's simply a little extra—not a tangible "suitcase full of cash." That's likely to be turned down. But money to the extent that money is for buying things . . . maybe you can acquire free travel, a dinner, or even a regular massage. (It pays to have employees in tip-top shape, right?) Ask for something out of scale, something that the other side can't afford or will raise eyebrows, and you've got a deal breaker, not something of benefit to your company. The bribe ideally should be something the other side doesn't mind throwing in, because it keeps you happy and coming back to them for more.

Of course, sometime down the road, the giving side may get tired of having to keep on giving. Parents don't want to keep handing out stickers every time a child goes potty after, say, age three and a half. The same goes for business. A business that is expected to keep handing out little gifts may want to break the habit at some point. Often, it's when new management comes in and is looking for ways to cut corners. Like the child who's outgrown the potty chair, you'll want to be aware of when you are getting too big to continue a practice that the other side no longer finds rewarding. It's best to be proactive about it and graciously and spontaneously give up accepting your "bribes" before you need to be asked.

Keep Coming Back to the Same Question

Children just never give up. Once they decide they want something, you know how stubborn they can be. They just come at you and keep coming at you until you've used up all your reasons why they can't have what they want. "Why can't I have a puppy?" You talk about your work schedule, your travel plans, the size of your yard, the cost of veterinary bills, and a million other reasons why it doesn't make sense for your family to own a dog. And yet somehow you still end up with that cute little cocker spaniel. And you know what—you're not sorry afterward. That's how all your neighbors ended up with their dogs, too.

Children are relentless about asking and asking and asking. Slowly but surely, they eliminate your defenses until you give them what they want.

Here's how one mother described her life:

My son tends to wear me down. I am using time-outs in the crib with some success. I give two verbal warnings, then on the third time, he goes in his crib for about ten minutes or until he simmers down. The problem is sometimes defining what is acceptable. For instance, I say "No throwing." Does dropping something deliberately count as throwing? My problem is also being consistent. Sometimes I am so frustrated, irritated, and fed up that enforcing time-outs becomes a problem in and of itself.

The same thing works in business. As long as you maintain a professional demeanor and you have something of substance to offer, you can, by asking and asking again, make slow inroads in the resistance the other side puts in your way. Sometimes businesses appreciate that you're persistent because if you pursue them so doggedly, that shows how effective you'll be as a partner, collaborator, or advocate.

Here's where a person's experience running marathons, or completing long cross-country ski trips, or having backpacked through the mountains with llamas and swum a mile a day, comes into play: Physical stamina counts. People assume that in negotiations it's cleverness, or having the right contacts, or business acumen, or mental toughness that will make the difference. To some degree that's true, but pure physical strength also counts for more than most people realize. Long meetings, hectic travel, eating on the run, fasting, hauling around projectors and papers, dashing around airports—these are not tasks for the physically weak or, dare I say it, obese. The sheer length of meetings and negotiations can determine who wins: The side with the most people still standing (or awake) may be the victor. The tired, exhausted, weary, drowsy, and fatigued negotiators lose in part because they've been worn down.

Staying trim and fit, getting ample sleep, and eating well are as important for business as they are for life. *Looking* fit—having a tan, a well-fitting suit, and so on—isn't the same. You need to be in good shape in order to wear the other side down and, just as important, not be worn down yourself. It would be a real shame to lose some negotiating points just because you're pooped.

Often it's impossible to tell when is the best time to strike a deal. You can't know the internal budget or priorities of the company you want to do business with: So, by asking on a regular basis, you increase your chance of hitting that company at the right moment.

Children learn from *The Little Engine That Could.* That book is the perfect how-to guide for being relentless. Defeat and losing are not possible, children learn, if they will unleash their boundless energy and self-confidence. I bet you never thought of that book as a business book, did you? Well, pick up a copy and give it a read. It only takes a minute but you may make its refrain, "I think I can, I think I can," into your mantra.

Play the Repeat Game

Here's something my kids like to do to drive each other crazy. My older daughter says something like, "It's my turn to play on the computer."

My younger daughter responds by parroting back those exact words: "It's my turn to play on the computer."

"No, it's not. It's *my* turn," says Karen.

"No, it's not. It's MY turn," echoes Claire.

"Stop repeating what I say," Karen sputters in frustration.

"Stop repeating what *I* say," Claire predictably spits back at her.

This exchange can go on for some time, until either a parent comes along and makes the repeater knock it off . . . or until the one whose words are being parroted gets sick of the game and flees to find some other activity, relinquishing the computer altogether so it is free for game-playing by her parrot-mouthed sister.

Is there an adult business application of this extremely juvenile technique? Yes, but it can't be copied at such a primitive level. If all you do is repeat the other side's statements, they'll think you're a lunatic and quickly conclude they can't do business with you at all. Translated into an adult negotiating technique, the purpose is not to drive your adversary insane and risk a punch in the mouth; the purpose is to use the other side's own words to emphasize those places where you are in agreement. This technique can help to move stalled negotiations forward, especially if you have detailed minutes or a transcript of a previous discussion at your disposal. Look over the notes or records carefully. Pull out those sentences and phrases that you can echo as your own, to show that you have enough of a common vision to keep moving forward. Rather than attempting to make the other side give up in frustration (which is usually the goal when a child of mine is at this game), you are trying to achieve just the opposite: to bring two widely separated positions closer together.

Let's say you're negotiating over a profit-sharing arrangement. The other side has made the point that the partner taking the greater risk should reap the largest share of the profits. You can agree to this position in principle, even as you continue to disagree about how risk is calculated. What you can do here is repeat that your side, too, believes that risk must be rewarded proportionately. But then you need to concentrate on the various types of risks that each side assumes. If you are convinced that the other side is trying to assume a greater share of the profits than is fair, point out those risks that your side is taking—less obvious risks, perhaps, that have not been given proper weight in the negotiations thus far—that deserve consideration. Now you are no longer divided over a matter of fundamental fairness, but are simply haggling over percentages. You can move forward from there.

Another technique that kids bring to this strategy is to change the emphasis over the words that they parrot back. Lawyers use this technique in court to great effect. In answer to a question, a witness says, "I saw the car dart across the intersection, and I braked, but

I couldn't avoid hitting it." The lawyer repeats the words back, emphasizing the words, "*And* I braked," to imply that the witness didn't start braking as he approached the intersection; he started braking only after he saw the other car. In other words, the other car was already in the intersection and had the right of way; it was his fault for noticing that too late.

One more little twist you can bring to the echo game: Change a word or a few words and see what effect you can get from it. If you want to see some great examples of this technique in action, watch some old episodes of *Perry Mason* from the 1950s and 1960s. The witness would swear, "I never asked him whether he changed his will. . . ." And Perry Mason would echo back, "You never *asked* . . ." and then go on to add the new words, in his most intimidating voice: "But isn't it true that you *saw* the new will? You never *asked* . . ." (*Big dramatic pause*) ". . . because you already *knew* . . ."

And in the show, of course, the witness is forced to echo the words, "Yes, yes, okay . . . I knew."*

---

* Results from this technique may vary widely. I cannot promise that it will work for you as well as it does for characters on TV shows.

Be Irrational

We tend to be prejudiced in favor of logical, mature behavior. But being irrational and unpredictable can have its place, believe it or not. Some of the biggest names in business—Richard Branson of Virgin Atlantic Airways leaps to mind—are proud of their reputations as wild men who are willing to walk the line and push things to extremes. In certain situations you can't let yourself be pigeonholed. It's better to be seen as a loose cannon, as someone who might do or say anything. When you're in danger of being pushed to the side, it might be just the right time to stand out, to do something risky, bold, and dramatic, something that makes the people around you sit up and take notice—anything to shake them up and make them realize they don't know you and can't chart out your responses for you. If you can come across as eccentrically brilliant (rather than just flaky), you can use irrationality to your advantage.

If people think there's a chance you might walk out in the middle of a project, then they'll work to keep you satisfied. Divas, movie stars, and Hollywood directors are all notorious for this sort of behavior (that is to say, behaving like irrational children), but when they have enough talent and charisma, they can get away with it. That is to say, it works.

But, to my mind, the champion of the "act irrational" technique was Richard Nixon, who worried that because he was weakened politically at home by the Watergate investigation, he would be perceived as vulnerable by his Soviet adversaries in the Kremlin. He was afraid they'd be emboldened to take advantage of his domestic distractions to foment insurrection in many Third World countries. So he allowed Henry Kissinger to start whispering to others that Nixon might do anything—including using nuclear weapons—against communist insurrection. The Soviets had to believe that Nixon was capable of doing *anything*. He was irrational, and irrational people should be treated with extreme caution. Release of Soviet files since the end of the Cold War proved Nixon correct: The Soviet leaders were worried that his response to certain actions might be out of proportion to the threat, and they trimmed their activities accordingly.

Acting irrationally may coax the other side into giving you want you want in order to prevent you from doing something *really* irrational. It goes without saying that you have to have the power to make people afraid that you can use it. That's why this technique, though often used by small children, rarely gets them anywhere. When a toddler is behaving irrationally, the adult can pick the child up and put her in her crib. When an adult is behaving irrationally—and that adult has real power over people's lives—people tend to do whatever's necessary to pacify the person.

The risk, it must be noted, is that those who perceive your behavior as dangerously irrational may feel compelled to remove you from a position of authority. That was certainly the case with Nixon. So if you employ this technique, you not only need to be sure that you currently have power to wield, but that you have the ability to hold onto it, even if others start working to pull you down.

Worry the Other Side That You Might Be Sick

"I don't feel so good, Mommy." With those words, many a child has stayed home from school or missed a piano lesson.

If they can't fake being sick, they can hold their breath until you worry that they'll faint. Anything to get their way. Let's not forget that kids also use "being sick" as a method of accumulating toys.

The same technique can succeed in business, too. When you get down to the nitty-gritty of business, you have to deal with individuals, not companies. People call in sick all the time, and in some cases, there's no question that it's just a negotiating technique. Ever heard of "blue flu"? That's a tactic that police unions have used that stops short of a strike. The officers don't all call in sick at once; just enough of them miss work each day to send the clear message to city administrators that there will be continuing manpower shortages until the union's salary demands are met.

In the book publishing business—my line of work—authors routinely say that they can't complete a manuscript on time because they're suffering from carpal tunnel syndrome, have back pain, or their spouse is in the hospital (they conveniently omit the fact that it's for a tummy tuck). Do writers have more illnesses than other people? Probably not. Do writers claim to get sick more than others? I can't speak to that . . . and I promise that *I've never used this technique*. I'm not advocating it, merely reporting something others have been known to use to their advantage.

As with so many of these child-inspired techniques, from acting irrationally to playing the forlorn victim role, you can't play the sick card too often. Overuse it and you'll be tagged as a malingerer. Make absolutely sure no one's going to see you at the baseball stadium on the day you've said you were stricken with the worst flu ever. You're generally better off going for a little-understood syndrome, one that can come and go mysteriously. That way, you can claim the need to fly home to see your specialist the day your negotiations reach the critical point, forcing the other side to accede to your demands or lose the deal.

Make Weak Promises

"If we get a dog, I promise to walk it." Thousands of parents recall their child's voice saying those exact words—as the parent walks the dog at 6:30 A.M. in the rain.

But it's not the child's fault, entirely: You knew, of course, that this was a false promise the moment you heard it. But hope nearly always triumphs over experience.

"I will clean up my room right after supper. I promise." And so you let your kids play outside for another half hour. And the room never gets cleaned. But you knew that, too.

In the book business, for example, publishers often make promises that they're not going to keep: "We will promote this book like crazy!" the publisher says. And authors, too, make their fair share of hollow promises: "I will get a foreword from a former United States President," the author says. Yes, of course, the author has sent off an e-mail asking the former President to do the foreword. And he certainly has the hope that the former President will say yes. Still, he's not entirely surprised when the answer turns out to be no. But by that time, the book contract is already signed and the book has taken up a slot in the fall release schedule. So the author goes for a substitute: a foreword from a former secretary of education. It doesn't exactly live up to the hype, but if it's a well-crafted piece, it's a fair enough substitute.

Making weak promises ranks among the riskiest of negotiating tactics.

The problem, from the vantage point of the party that's on the receiving end of them, is that we want so much to reach an agreement that we give in. Even when we know deep down that the other side is not likely to abide by the agreement, we sometimes give in just to get the process over with.

When you are on the offering end of a weak promise, you risk losing credibility, so make sure that there is something in the deal that you can, in fact, abide by. You don't want to completely break your promise or go back on your word because that's a reputation that will shadow you forever. You absolutely want to be able to point to promises you've kept. So, if you promise a foreword written by an ex-President, be sure you've got that former cabinet secretary already lined up to call on as a backup.

Win Through Cuteness

When you look into a child's face you *have* to say yes. When they blink their wide eyes, you have to say okay to everything. Children were designed to cause parents to become weak at the knees. From the moment they're born to their first smile, to when they say "Mama and Dada" for the first time—they're adorable. Even when children do things like spill a glass of milk on the floor or knock over your antique vase, you forgive them in an instant because they look so guileless and endearing. But don't think they don't know that.

How can you translate that quality into a sound business practice?

It sounds glib to suggest that you send in your most physically attractive negotiators, but that's exactly what can help. People react better to beautiful individuals than to plain ones, as has been demonstrated in countless psychology experiments. You know the setup: The sales script is exactly the same and the speech is delivered at the same pace, with the same gestures, but the target audience in one room hears the presentation from a man who's six feet tall, well dressed, well groomed, and movie-star handsome; the target audience in the other room hears the pitch from someone with, let's just say, a much less appealing presence. It's no surprise that the test group that heard the pitch from the handsome salesman buys more every time. Perhaps you will be surprised to learn that women care just as much about the looks of the salesman as men seem to care about the looks of saleswomen.

Is there hope, then, for the noncute among us? Glossy magazines would have us believe that anybody can be made to look appealing. While physically attractive men and women enjoy certain advantages, there are lots of ways to make somebody appear attractive, interesting, attention-grabbing, desirable, or popular. Turn your negotiators into winning-*looking* negotiators.

Grown-ups can be cute. It's often a matter of smiling a lot more than you're used to, or wearing a brighter color than usual, or having something fun or funky on your lapel. If you outfit yourself entirely from Brooks Brothers, you don't have much hope at being able to use your looks as a negotiating tool.

Do you really think that famed defense attorney Gerry Spence is that great a lawyer? Or could his success possibly, just possibly, have something to do with the fact that he's not a conventional dresser? (He's the one with the shaggy head of longish white hair, who always wears a fringed leather cowboy jacket with a bolo tie in the courtroom.)

You must be comfortable in your own style. Gerry Spence does fine with his western look, but I doubt that he'd be as formidable in polyester. Think about what you're wearing, how you look (even men can make use of makeup), how you walk, how you smile, how you speak. Get coached if you want or need to—and virtually everyone can use a speech coach to learn some presentation pointers. If you think that coaching is a waste of time, consider this: Your opponent might be getting coached. Persuasion involves performance, and it helps to remember Shakespeare:

All the world's a stage,
And all the men and women merely players.
They have their exits and their entrances;
And one man in his time plays many parts.

When you're in the midst of a serious negotiation (and all negotiations are serious), become immersed in your role. *Look* the part, just as children do.

Not every use of this technique is aimed at winning, however. One parent told me that her child "will smile and giggle, then get silly when I ask him not to do something. It's a test." This technique can be used to probe your opponent, which in fact can be a somewhat more sophisticated use of "cuteness." It goes without saying that the more you know about the other side, the better a position you'll be in when it comes time to actually negotiate. Intelligence—get it.

One big caution here is that cuteness alone is never enough (except perhaps when we're talking about babies). If it were, then you'd just send in the best-looking person in your outfit to be your point person every time. *Not* a good idea. But put a team together that has both beauty and brains, and there's a winning combination. Sometimes companies don't send either on a mission, and that's a sure recipe for losing the negotiation.

Don't Fear Failure

There are two kinds of people: Those who watch adventure documentaries on television and those who actually do things like snowboard on Mount Everest, fly airplanes upside down at 200 mph, and swim with great white sharks. There are those of us who are normal and those of us who are fearless. Fearless people can do things that normal people can't.

And so it is with children. Sure, some children are more fearful than adults, but childhood fear is a different sort of thing. Children know fear because there are ghosts, skeletons, monsters under the bed, and thunder. But the one thing that children are not afraid of is failure. When their egos are still young and underdeveloped, they haven't yet begun to focus on questions like, "What will people think of me if I lose?" or "Will I end up looking ridiculous if I fail?" That's an adult kind of fear, and it's something that holds adults back from trying things they might turn out to be good at. Kids aren't so burdened with thoughts of reputation. They don't worry about what goes in their file; they aren't concerned about a loss of prestige, power, or face. And this quality gives them a great deal of power when it comes to negotiating.

Analyze an intense negotiation over bedtime between a parent and child. The parent is worried about setting a bad precedent and losing "power" over the child if she gives in. Parents will freely admit that. Does that mean that the parent is going to be more dogged when it comes to the negotiations? Perhaps. But what it also means is that the child can extract compromises. The child says, "If I can't stay up late, can I at least watch an episode of *Blue's Clues?*" Or, "I'll go to bed, but can I have another bedtime story first?" This inner boldness that comes from not caring about one's image is something that all children, but few adults, have.

How do you achieve this state, this ability not to fear failure? It is something that probably can't be explained in a book of any length. Only by experiencing fearlessness in some area of your life can you incorporate that spirit in your negotiating repertoire. Am I suggesting that you start climbing mountains or learning to pilot an airplane? Absolutely! Piloting a plane is something I will recommend to you personally—it's given me great confidence in my own abilities and unquestionably broadened my sense of what I can accomplish. Taking up an adventure sport is something that's worked to give many people a depth of perspective that helps them negotiate without the fear of failure.

An adventure that gives you a new sense of boldness does not have to come in the form of a death-defying activity that automatically cancels your life insurance. Standing in front of an audience performing karaoke, watching a somber documentary or two (if all you ever see on the screen are action thrillers), taking a class in something you've never studied before, exploring a wing of a museum that's been invisible to you all these years, these are the kinds of things that can help you break out of your cocoon.

Be Prepared—But Not Overprepared

Children are often caught unprepared. That's okay for them, because adults think that's something they'll learn as they grow up and come to understand the consequences of being unprepared. Or they think it's something their kids will pick up if they become Boy Scouts or Girl Scouts, as part of the movement's ideology. I'm not about to knock preparedness as a good life lesson. There's no question that it's a virtue in most business negotiations. But while acquiring habits of good preparation, adults sometimes lose one of the virtues of childhood: their spontaneity. Kids have an innate liveliness about them. They are bubbly and show enthusiasm and are able to think on their feet—qualities that have a tendency to fade away as they mature. And that's a shame.

You know what kids do when they're not prepared for class? They're often funny and inventive in their excuses for why they're not prepared. The kid with little imagination claims "The dog ate my homework," and the teacher groans at the same old line. The kid who says, "I know my dog didn't eat it—I just wish I knew what he did with it," at least has some freshness to his response.

(He may still be marked down for not having done the assignment, though.) But sometimes a truly novel and unusual response can win a reprieve. Here's an approach that, depending on the teacher and subject, might stand a bit of a chance: "I wanted to write that book report, but I realized I just couldn't come up with anything new or important to say. I thought it was better to admit that than to hand in something inferior."

When an adult is unprepared (and despite our best intentions, there will always come a time when we find ourselves in that situation), the tendency is to flounder around, come up with lame excuses, and make things worse. A common reaction is to blame others; but that almost always has repercussions, hurting teamwork. Some adults think they can wing it, pass themselves off as prepared, either by good guesswork or by drawing on some past experience that makes them seem prepared when they're not. Here's where it might help to have retained a bit of childlike spunk and spontaneity. See what you can come up with—or as they say in the military, when they're not sure how something might fly, "Run it up the flagpole and see who salutes."

It's the rare adult that can face up to the situation squarely and say, "Sorry, I'm unprepared. My fault." That's undoubtedly the most mature—but least childlike—thing to do.

You've Won—Now You Have to Win Your Friends Back

What is amazing about children is how extreme enemies can become friends again. It's almost like a broken bone being mended, the way kids can repair their relationships. The renewed friendship can be better, stronger, than it was to begin with. Of course, children have several advantages over adults when it comes to undoing bad relationships: They usually don't brood over the problem all evening after work, and they have lots of school breaks and family time—time apart from the other child that can help mend the wound.

I'm not suggesting that all childhood animosities are forgotten, only that chances of that happening are better among children than adults. And unfortunately, I can't prescribe a method for turning adversaries back into friends, since human relationships are as complex as they are varied. But what I am saying is that adults can learn from children how to put aside their grudges and move on.

It could be that if you apply—or perhaps, misapply—some of the advice in this book, you will step on some people's toes. Oftentimes people feel they've been hurt when one person gets ahead, even if that person has done nothing wrong. Adults are touchier than children; they're quicker to perceive slights. (They're definitely more litigious.) One of the things all children are supposed to learn to do is to say "sorry" when an apology is called for. But that's something that few children and even fewer adults ever learn to do well. Children may be prompted to mumble the word *sorry* insincerely. Adults learn to pack in a few excuses and self-justifications while delivering the apology: "I'm sorry if you were offended by what I said, even though it was meant to be taken ironically. I guess I didn't realize that anyone could take what I said so literally." (In other words, it's your own fault for being such a stodgy, humorless twit.)

A truly great gift for someone in a leadership position to have is the ability to know when an apology is called for and to deliver it simply, without caviling or embellishment, without cravenness or condescension: Just a simple and sincere, "I'm sorry."

This is one of those things I wish they'd teach in business school, for all those adults who have come through every grade in school, from kindergarten onward, and have never managed to learn how to do it right.

You've Lost—Now Don't Be a Sorehead

Win or lose, children move on. They get over it.

In other words, children grow from their experiences. They may not be able to intellectualize what they've learned, but this lack of ability to dwell on the past is also a plus for them, because they're not so apt to get caught up in a cycle of asking, "What went wrong?" They're short-term focus is their strength.

Three things are likely to happen when children lose:

1. They cry.

2. They go on to something else.

3. They forget about it.

Let's look at each of these reactions one at a time. Adults often *want* to cry; children frequently do. Crying isn't always a bad thing to do (earlier I explained why)—although it's not a negotiating strategy I would say you should make part of your usual repertoire.

Crying doesn't tend to go over well at the negotiating table, and it certainly doesn't hasten the day that you're going to occupy that corner office.

But crying does do some useful things for children, which are worth keeping in mind. The main thing it does is help the child dry out emotionally. Children cry because they feel sad. Adults feel sad, but don't cry—and they may not have developed any other way to let their sad feelings out. Well, they may drink, but that's seldom a productive outlet, is it? I don't know why getting drunk when you lose isn't more stigmatized than crying in public; certainly the consequences for the people around you can be worse, especially if nobody's managed to take away your car keys. But, for some reason, most guys would rather be seen stumbling around drunk after a bad day at the office than sitting quietly at the desk, head in both hands, with tears escaping from the corners of their eyes. I say both children and adults need to find an outlet for their negative emotions. If crying does the trick, then cry—though it may be worthwhile to learn to hold back the tears till you're in a private place, or at least among very good friends.

What about moving on to something else? Children have so many things going on in their lives—it's as if their lives are comprised of a hundred mini-projects and that within minutes of not getting what they wanted, they're on to something else. They have no choice about it. Adults are usually not as lucky, since we tend to work on just one or two projects at a time. It's often our misfortune that we're required to do a postmortem, to write a report about what went wrong. Occasionally that's a helpful exercise, such as when it's not clear why a deal fell through. But more often than not, we *know* what we did wrong. Taking the time to spell it out is just rubbing our noses in it. It's painful and unnecessary. Think back to when you were a kid and you blurted out some inappropriate response in class and were made to write a hundred times on a sheet of paper "I will not talk in class" or some other recantation. Did that help? Of course not! It just left you with a sense of futility and a hand cramp. A brief chat with the teacher after class would be much better, because then the teacher would have a chance to tell you, privately but sternly, why your outburst was disruptive, and you'd have a chance to apologize simply but sincerely (as discussed in the preceding chapter).

Then again, adult mistakes tend to be more serious than the wrong word tossed out in a class full of kids with short memories. Kids move on because their mistakes don't matter as much. When you've blown a negotiation that was supposed to land your company a multimillion-dollar contract, you probably won't be able to put the whole episode behind you quite as quickly as the child who's made a boo-boo at school. We get to let everything that didn't go right during the negotiations roll around in our brains from the moment we put our head on the pillow until, say, 4 A.M. Don't you envy being a kid?

You need to keep telling yourself that if you dwell on your past problems—or more significantly, *let others dwell on your past problems*—you will have a hard time shaking your association with that failure. Your best shot at changing your status is to get yourself associated with other, better outcomes. Put the misery behind you as quickly as possible, move forward into something else, and focus on that task. As they say in Hollywood, "You're only as good as your next big hit." For someone coming off a project that wasn't a hit, that's actually a positive thought. Your next success is the surest way to cancel out a past failure.

Now, what about just forgetting about it? (Or, as we New Yorkers are famous for saying, "Fuggedaboutit!") If you are able to follow the advice to quickly move on to something else and you manage to make it to the end of "the next big thing," and this time with success, people will let you forget. Yes, you may encounter the occasional needler who just won't let go of your flop from the past, and you may feel like looking for some fast way to make him wipe that sneer right off his smug puss—but if you do, then what are you? A sorehead. Magnanimity is called for when dealing with people who would try to taunt you about the past. You turn away with a shrug as if to say, "This too shall pass." Remember that many of the Wright brothers' early airplane models ended up smashed to smithereens. They didn't let the naysayers slow them down.

Optimism Rules

There's more to learning to negotiate like a child than what's encompassed in the specific techniques discussed in this book. Leveraging tantrums, appearing naive, playing by the rules, and so on are important, but without understanding what the essence of childhood is, these techniques are just tricks and gimmicks. You may be like the bad actor in a B-grade movie: just moving your lips and saying your lines without any ability to improvise. Memorizing these techniques isn't what negotiating like a child is really about.

They way children view life gives them strength that adults no longer enjoy. Just as kids' bodies are able to repair themselves after an accident with incredible speed and apparent ease, children's minds operate in a way that gives them considerable negotiating vigor. It's not just the negotiating techniques that are important—it's the way children's brains work that makes them such negotiating powerhouses. In other words, the techniques that I've been talking about in this book are an integral part of being a kid. It is childhood itself that makes these techniques possible.

You can use any and all of these various techniques—throw a

tantrum, win through cuteness, take your ball and go home, be nice—but they are just isolated tools unless you learn to think like a child. Or rather, think *once again* like a kid. Children's bodies and minds are strong and resilient. Witness a child's ability to resist drowning. Children can stay submerged under water for prolonged periods of time and still be okay. There's one documented case of a child being submerged for seventy minutes and surviving. Adult brains lose this resilience, I'm sorry to report.

Adults long to be youthful. But we long to be youthful of body, not necessarily of mind. Plastic surgery for drooping body parts; creams and ointments to rejuvenate skin; potions for silkier hair—we buy such procedures and products to the tune of $160 billion a year worldwide. We fret over how old we're looking; we spend hours putting on makeup. Advertising promotes these things like almost nothing else. (Except for automobiles, perhaps. But when you think about it, what's the main theme of automobile advertising: youth and power.) I would bet that most adults over the age 40 spend at least a significant portion of each day thinking about and/or doing something about looking younger.

And to some degree we succeed. Cosmetic surgery works. Makeup works. Skin creams and shampoos can achieve their promises, if only for a limited time. Health clubs and exercise equipment (which weren't even included in the $160 billion figure) also take up much of our money and time—and again, to make us look and feel younger.

But what about our attitude and approach to life? What about our minds? At a lot of health clubs, you can pound the treadmill while watching CNN. But if what you're trying to do is look and feel younger, wouldn't it be better to have all of those televisions tuned to classic TV—*Leave It to Beaver, Bewitched,* and *Mayberry RFD*? Watch a movie like *Big,* starring Tom Hanks. Don't waste your time watching what kids watch today, especially sitcoms that show kids as miniature grown-ups, all smart-mouthed and sexy. Watch the old black-and-white kids' shows on Nickelodeon to see what it was like when being a kid meant being innocent, not ironic. Kids used to be fresh and full of curiosity, not "full of it." There are some exceptions, of course, but as a general rule of thumb, classic television from the 1960s does a much better job of showing how children actually negotiate.

Decades ago Rod Serling wrote a story, "Kick the Can," in which several elderly residents of a seniors' boarding house decide one day to play a children's game called kick the can, something they enjoyed when they were kids. They start running around (well, sort of, since one person is in a wheel chair), kicking a can, yelling, hooting, and otherwise acting childish. There's one holdout, however: a curmudgeonly old man who stubbornly refuses to engage in these juvenile antics.

The others go on playing kick the can without inhibition. While they have fun, the curmudgeon stays in his room, trying not to listen to the running around. Then the noises change from wispy, out-of-breath shouts to high-pitched squeals. His friends have changed: They've been transformed into children, with their whole childhood to enjoy again. They were transformed through the magic of their minds.

I'm not suggesting that you dispense with being an adult and act like a kid all the time. People who do that end up working behind the counter in computer game stores, so my advice is not meant for the most literal interpretation. What I am suggesting is that you develop a partnership with your childhood. That you reach back into time and bring back those things that gave you power: optimism, energy, spontaneity, a sense of adventure, looking at the world in new ways.

Generally—and perhaps universally—speaking, children are happier far more often than adults. "Today is the best day of my whole entire life," Katy says to her aunt who's baby-sitting, according to the words of a Christine Lavin song. As they swirl and twirl around the living room, the aunt is thrilled to hear her niece say that she's never had a better day in the three years she's been alive. When Katy's parents come home and her aunt relates this story to them, the parents smile and say that she says this about almost every day of her life. Nearly every day is a great day for a child because children have the capacity—and desire—to enjoy life. Happiness translates into enthusiasm and potency. When you're "up," you're going to be better at negotiating. If you're feeling down, depressed, disheartened, or glum, the other side's going to walk all over you. You can't out-negotiate the person who knows how to discover what's best and most wonderful about everything in life.

I'll admit that it's not that easy to recapture the mind-set of being a child. While children suffer from anxiety and stress, they suffer much less than adults. Children don't worry about money, disease, leaking roofs, neighbor problems, parking tickets, or grades at school or work. Mostly their lives are carefree because they have fewer responsibilities and fewer rules than adults. They have it easy.

Oddly, few kids are aware that they have it so good. They have no way to compare the freedom and playfulness of childhood with what's around the corner: The real world. The real world is a universe apart; another dimension that they can't even begin to fathom. You may think that kids really want to hear the answers when they ask you, "Why? Why? Why?" about what goes on in the adult world, but more often than not, they're asking just to ask. Your detailed attempts to explain why you have to file taxes or what happens when a court case is appealed sail right over the head of the eight-year-old, despite his apparent burning curiosity just moments before. You may turn around and discover he's already gone off to ask somebody else another question entirely.

Children rarely have a sense of foreboding, of pessimistic doom. They are filled with optimism. My oldest daughter, Karen, has—or had during her toddler years—three special blankets. One by one, she lost them, until there was only one soft green blankie left. You have to understand that for Karen, her blanket was the most precious thing in the world. Yet even after she lost two and had only the one left, she couldn't conceive of leaving the remaining one safe at home. She always insisted on bringing it along on trips and outings. Pessimist adults that we were, we warned her darkly that she could lose her last and only blankie—no, probably *would* lose it, just as she's lost the other two. *We* feared Karen losing her blanket, but she never had any such worry! While our fear was sensible, and her lack of fear irrational, we were the ones suffering stress while Karen was blithely oblivious to our gloom. And she turned out to be right. She has that symbol of toddler hope to this day as proof.

"There's a right way and there's a wrong way." "Don't ask stupid questions." "Experts are always right." "Don't be silly." "Don't make a mistake." These are rules adults live by. They are rules that children violate nearly every waking minute. There often is an alternative way to do something; asking stupid questions can yield new insights; experts are often wrong; being silly can be liberating from the pressures of conformity; and sometimes mistakes have led to the most brilliant insights and great discoveries.

Everything is a toy to children: empty cheese wheels, inkless pens, expensive watches, swivel chairs (*especially swivel chairs*), television remote controls, dandelions in a field. Children have the extraordinary capability to turn mundane objects into play things. Like some "matter transformer" out of a science fiction story, children can transmute the dull and ordinary into the fun and energizing. When everything has the potential to become something else—that's imagination.

Tapping Into Your Childhood's Power

At the risk of invoking another cliché, kids not only think outside the box, their entire world is outside the box. Their vision is pure, uninhibited, and intelligent in ways that most adults can no longer comprehend. Imagination is the underlying theme behind children's special negotiating powers.

How do you tap into your childhood's power? I wish all you had to do was gather your old friends and play a round of kick the can. I wish I could give you step-by-step instructions on how to rejoin your childhood. But I can't—in part because everyone's journey backward takes a path that's determined by their own life and experiences. If you grew up as an army brat, spending time in this and that town, your childhood and early adulthood may be very different from somebody who spent their formative years growing up in downtown Chicago. That's why a chapter on how to restore the vigor, imagination, vitality, curiosity, and inner strength of childhood is impossible. Your path back to your childhood strength and power is unique to you. I can only offer general guidelines and the reason.

I've talked about various things you can do to develop a child's eye view of the world and thereby help develop your negotiating skills. Reading about these skills isn't sufficient; you need the practical experience that the connection to children can bring. Here are a few ways to get that experience:

• *Spend more time with children.* Start with your own children, if you have them. If you're not a parent or if your children are grown, borrow some. (I do mean that figuratively, not literally.) Take them someplace that's fun for you and for them, but don't be too forward or controlling. Hang back a bit, watch, and listen. If you don't have any young nieces, nephews, grandchildren, or godchildren, then be sure to keep an eye out for children you may observe in your day-to-day activities. Shopping. In the park. At the bus stop. In line at the movies. It's especially useful to watch children in places where they are prone to do a lot of negotiating, such as on airplane flights. (If you're on a cross-country flight where the toddler behind you is kicking your seat for hours without end, turn the situation from a stressful event into an educational experience.) Transportation venues in general—trains, highway rest stops, airport waiting areas, and ticket lines—present many situations to observe how children negotiate.

• *Allow playfulness back into your life.* I know, you golf. You watch the World Series. You explore a new section of the Louvre every time you visit Paris. But that's not acting childlike. Those kinds of activities don't do anything to restore your sense of wonder and fire up your imagination. Well, what *should* you do? Go out and have fun for the sake of fun.

Obviously, running around, kicking a can with your friends isn't going to happen. (But why not?) If you can't overcome the fear of looking silly in public (which almost all grown-ups have), then try something that's a little less, well, embarrassing. Play a game of Monopoly, or Chutes and Ladders. Play Paint Ball. Go orienteering—a navigation competition that's sort of the adult version of hide and seek. It's fun, often challenging, and good exercise.* Instead of "real" golf, try a round of miniature golf every once in a while. Reread a favorite book from your childhood. Listen to the songs you grew up loving and used to play over and over.

It's surprising how many adults don't listen to music anymore. When did we stop? The answer to that question is probably around

---

* For more information about orienteering, visit www.online-orienteering.net or www.us.orienteering.org.

when we got serious about our work: when we were angling for partner at the law firm; when the VP of marketing position was within our sights; when we knew that we might become the director of operations. Why did we stop? You'll have to answer that question. But as you try and answer it, my guess is that you won't have a good answer. Why did you enjoy listening to the Beatles, the Beach Boys, the Spice Girls, and then one day no longer enjoy it? If you don't have a good answer to that question, then go back to listening to music once again. And better still, look for *new* music. There are countless bands and musicians in every musical genre, and probably some genres you haven't even heard of. Finding new music is easy (easier than most things), and it may pave the way for you to explore other areas that invigorate your imagination, boost your energy, and give you insights that you never had (and that the people you're negotiating with don't have, either.)*

• *Look at the everyday, familiar things in your routine with an eye toward seeing something new and inspiring.* At some time everything is brand-new to children. But some things—seeing a butterfly alight on a flower, for example—can be new only once. Or can it? You have never seen that particular butterfly alight on that exact petal of that particular flower before, have you? Nothing when investigated is ever completely the same as another thing. There's always more than meets the eye . . . when you know how to look for it.

For a child, each new object, event, animal, insect, food, sound, smell brings forth an endless stream of questions. Children only articulate a small fraction of what they are thinking, because they are too captivated by what they see to think too hard about it.

---

* Here are some of my favorite places to start looking for new music. No matter what you like, or liked to listen to once upon a time, these three Web sites— www.cdbaby.com, www.musicaldiscoveries.com, and www.ecto.org—will stimulate your "imagivision."

Seeing the world in new ways, seeing new things, is a vital aspect of knowing how to negotiate like a child.

If everything you know comes from *The Wall Street Journal* and *Business Week,* then you're probably not a creative person. But if you look at the world from the perspective that there's going to be something new to learn, then chances are you're going to come up with new ideas on how to win the negotiation. So when the delegation from China comes to the pre-negotiation reception, be friendly, step right up, and ask questions. Ask about their homes and families. Politely, of course. You don't want to come across as nosy. But you want to be friendly while you learn whatever you can about the people who will be on the opposite side of the table from you for the next week of talks. And not just because you want to gain an advantage. You want to know because it's good to know things. Because you have retained that childlike curiosity about the world that you had when the world was new to you.

Back to the Beginning

If you want to outnegotiate your opponent, you have to go back to the beginning, the basics. Recall the technique that you successfully used to get your parents to push you in the stroller when you really could walk. Remember how you got your parents to let you have a candy bar before dinner, even though everyone knew that it really would ruin your appetite. Think about the technique you used to convince your parents to let you stay up late to watch your favorite television show, or how you got your friend Jenny to let you borrow her sweater, or how you got a pet dog that you never walked after the first day. Those techniques worked back then and can work now, provided you recognize and incorporate them into your adult life by becoming a bit of a child again.

If I had to summarize *How to Negotiate Like a Child* in a single word, it would be imagination. That is what this book is about—expanding your imagination and your ability to innovate, think on your feet, improvise, and develop brand-new solutions to vexing problems. The power of imagination will give you an undeniable advantage over your negotiating partners, most of whom are using old, tired playbooks that stick to strict rules and procedures.

I know it's easy to talk about imagination, creativity, and the ability to think quickly and adapt. It's almost a cliché to say that these things will give you an edge in negotiations. But I wouldn't have written this book if I thought I was just dishing out some shopworn stuff you've heard plenty of times before. It's one thing to know about stuff; it's another to know when and how to use it.

I fly airplanes. Most of the time, flying airplanes is an easy thing. All those buttons, knobs, and gauges can pretty much be ignored because flying is mostly a matter of keeping the airplane moving fast enough so that there's enough airflow over and under the wings to keep the plane aloft. Sometimes things go wrong. There's bad weather; ice forms on the wings; or something's the matter with the fuel. Then that airport, which is only ten miles away, might as well be a thousand miles away. You smell something strange coming out of the engine compartment: Now what do you do?

Well, you can read all about it. Pilots read aviation publications all the time. But reading or listening to a lecture about something is vastly different from actually practicing it. Reading can enlighten you intellectually, but reading alone does not translate into practical benefits. Only "doing" allows you to master a skill. Before I ever performed a simulated emergency landing in an airplane, I read about dozens of them. I memorized the steps and had them down cold. What happened when my instructor pulled the power and I was on my own? I messed up about 25 percent of those steps. Only after doing several simulated emergency landings did I manage to get it right. Business and aviation skills are different, of course: Aviation involves both studied skills and physical skills, whereas in business, you're rarely required to be able to do anything physically.

But the general principle applies: You can't just expect to read something and be able to master or apply it.

The techniques in *How to Negotiate Like a Child* must be brought into your business way of life, or else they'll vanish and reading this book will have been a waste of time (although you'll have enjoyed my sparkly humor). That brings me back to the book's kernel, which I mentioned just a moment ago: Deploy your imagination. But don't just tell yourself that you're going to be more imaginative, creative, and innovative: Do it. Start using these techniques. If you're reading this book because you are in the world of business where negotiations occur in one form or another a dozen times a day, it makes sense to start using these techniques right away.

Kids are successful negotiators in part because they're fearless and will try all kinds of new things without stopping to think of the reasons not to try them. How often have you seen a kid dive into a swimming pool and do a belly flop? And then he gets back up and tries the dive again and belly flops again, or back flops instead. Sooner or later the kid gets the dive right, and then soon after that, he tries a back flip. It's all fun to the kid, too. Even falling on your face in front of a lot of people is fun. That's the spirit I admire most about kids. It's their willingness to mess up that I love best about them. If only we adults had that freedom from the pressure of our own expectations!

In other words, kids generally operate stress-free. Even when they seem to be exploding with stress—throwing a tantrum—they seem to be throwing the stress out. Once the tantrum has passed, they're cleansed of stress. A lack of stress gives children incredible strength. Indeed, the absence of stress (which is the kind of worry, angst, and anxiety that causes adults to drink, take pills, and spend hours in therapy) goes a long way toward explaining why a child can get away with so many of these techniques that an adult just can't manage to pull off. Sorry, but it's a rare fifty-year-old who can wheedle and charm his way into getting a deadline extended for the third time. He's just too worried the other side will see through him to give it a go. (He's probably right, too.) The child, having not learned from experience to worry about failure, just does it. And wins.

Using these techniques may not bring you to a complete state of childlike absence of stress, but the more you act like a carefree child, the more you may feel childlike in spirit—and that is an incredibly important thing. Just as an absence of stress is useful, being stressed can dramatically reduce your chances of coming out on top in negotiations. Stress clouds your mind more than alcohol or drugs. Stress makes it *impossible* to think clearly, to tap into your creativity, to figure out what you need to do next. The more stressed you are, the more likely you are to fail—and fail big time. Study after study among pilots clearly confirms this fact: When under great stress, pilots make bad decisions and miss opportunities to make good decisions. No matter how good the pilot, stress (and believe me, all pilots feel stress and fear at some point) adversely affects a pilot. The same is true for other professions and activities, whether you are practicing medicine, driving a car, climbing rocks, or restocking grocery store shelves. Aviation is just better studied, and there's better data. Lack of sleep gets a good deal of press as a factor that adversely impacts decision making and overall cognitive ability. Yet stress, which is often harder to quantify, may be even more of a problem.

There are lot of techniques (and prescription drugs, apparently) that can help lower your stress level. Over the past decade numerous books have been written about dealing with stress, not to mention countless magazine and newspaper articles. You can choose from a dozen or more meditative techniques, or you can select the yoga style of your choice to help reduce your stress level. It's not my purpose here to give you pointers on how to reduce stress, other than to say that the more you can incorporate a child's perspective, the less stress you will feel. That's not to say that children can never get stressed (obviously, that's not so), but when they do they tend to be able to throw it off quickly and bounce back faster. Children are mostly happy, playful, inquisitive, fun-oriented, and cheerful (despite what the guests who appear on morning talk shows have to say). When was the last time you saw a four-year-old not being able to fall asleep because he was worried about something in preschool?

If nothing else, behaving a little more like a child and a little less like an adult will help clear your head and make you a more innovative, energetic, and successful negotiator.

There's one other wonderful thing about children, too. All the possibilities are limitless to them. Any single deal is sometimes an all-or-nothing venture. There's no make-or-break point because they haven't yet learned to define themselves by whether they succeed or fail at whatever they attempt. We adults, who get so bound up in our work that we stress out over it and feel devastated by setbacks, are the ones who need to change. We need to unlearn our self-defeating lessons and go back to the child's sense of boundlessness. When you know you can always try something anew, start over, do better next time, you have confidence in yourself and enjoy what you're doing.

On the opposite side of the coin, someone who feels bound by rules on all sides, unable to maneuver, and afraid to take a risk is someone whose buttons you can push to get the results you want. That's not even a negotiation; it's like playing against a crude computer game with limited memory and limited processor capability. When you're bursting with life and could go off in any of a million ways, have lots of energy and strategies in reserve, and a sense that even if you fail, you can still come back with a new and better idea, then you bring real power to the table. And that is how to negotiate like a child.

Index